DISCIPLES

OF

THE BUDDHA

DISCIPLES
OF
THE BUDDHA

LIVING IMAGES OF MEDITATION

by

ROBERT NEWMAN

Cool Grove Press - Zangdokpalri Editions

Published in the United States by Cool Grove Press,
an imprint of Cool Grove Publishing, Inc., New York.
512 Argyle Road, Brooklyn, NY 11218
http://WWW.COOLGROVE.COM

Publishers Cataloging-in-Publication

Newman, Robert, 1935-
Disciples of the Buddha : living images of meditation / by Robert Newman ; introduction by Chogyam Trungpa. -- 1st ed.
p. cm.
Includes bibliographical references.
LCCN: 00-130474
ISBN: 1-887276-20-3 (Hard)
ISBN: 1-887276-21-1 (Paper)

1. Meditation--Buddhism--In art. 2. Art, Buddhist. 3. Buddhist art and symbolism. 4. Arhats. I. Title.

N8193.N49 2000 704.948'943'435
QBI00-256

First Edition
Printed in China

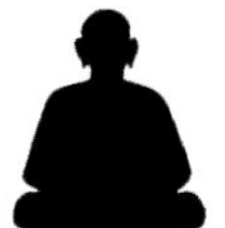

Contents

Preface x

Dedication
by H. H. Dudjom Rinpoche, Jigdral Yeshe Dorje xiii

Introduction by Chögyam Trungpa 1

Living Images of Meditation 30

Arhats in Scripture and Literature 47

Imagery of Life Devoted
to the Inner Way 66

Arhats in the Tibetan Tradition 84

The Torch of Precious Jewels
Sadhana of the Buddha and Sixteen Arhats
by H. H. Dudjom Rinpoche, Jigdral Yeshe Dorje 87

Notes on the Torch of Precious Jewels 130

Glossary 134

Selected Bibliography 139

Data 142

Location 144

Dates 145

Illustration Credits 146

Acknowledgements 149

Preface

In the Presence of the Buddha

CH'AN (ZEN) is a lineage of the Buddha, with the awakened state as its basis. Ch'an means meditation, sitting to awaken. The practice of sitting into the presence of the inherent awake state is central to the training. There's an instant shift to inherent Buddhanature.* This meditation practice lineage developed into a great spiritual order in China, continuing for many centuries and it continues in Japan and the West. The I-Chou Lohan statues, characterizations of direct disciples of Shakyamuni Buddha, represent Ch'an at the height of its influence in China. The Disciples, referred to as arhats in Sanskrit and lohans in Chinese, bring us face to face with images of a living tradition devoted to awakening and care.

In the Ch'an scriptures there's a famous four-line stanza attributed to Bodhidharma but maybe formulated much later:

A special tradition outside the scriptures;
No dependence on concept or language;
Direct pointing at the essence of awareness;
Seeing into one's nature and the return to buddhahood.†

At the inception of this lineage, legend has it that Shakyamuni Buddha smiled while holding up a flower, indicating inherent openness, and his close disciple Kasyapa recognized his own Buddhanature, the essence of Buddha Dharma, the seat of liberation. The first holder of "The Lamp of Transmission", Kasyapa, is said to have transmitted the essential recognition to the Buddha's close disciple Ananda, in a communication in which there was superknowledge beyond words.

---

* Buddhanature: The inherent awakened nature of human beings and all sentient life.

† Adapted from various translations

In China, Ananda and Kasyapa were the first disciples depicted in art, usually at the sides of the Buddha. Bodhidharma is called the Twenty-eighth Patriarch in India. He alone is said to have brought the lineage to China about 520 AD. Considered something of a radical by Buddhist institutions then present, the legends say that Bodhidharma practiced meditation by facing a wall for nine years.

The posture of sitting meditation (dhyana asana, skt.) brings psychological balance and stability, a willingness to stay open, spacious, not identifying with the display of mind. It's said that Bodhidharma brought PI-KUAN, "wall gazing"—an extended sitting meditation practice inspired by inherent Buddhahood.

The recognition of inherent Buddhahood was the basis of the union of the holder of "the lamp" with the next destined patriarch. A great lineage of transmission was present for centuries in China and then in Japan and continues today. Like Ch'an, Dzogchen and Mahamudra lineages of Tibetan Vajrayana Buddhism also continue today as living traditions of the meditative path.

The I-Chou Lohan statues are images of the Awakened One's direct disciples, the first practitioners to experience the fruit of the path revealed by the historical Buddha. They're images of awakened individuals. They introduce us to our awakened state.

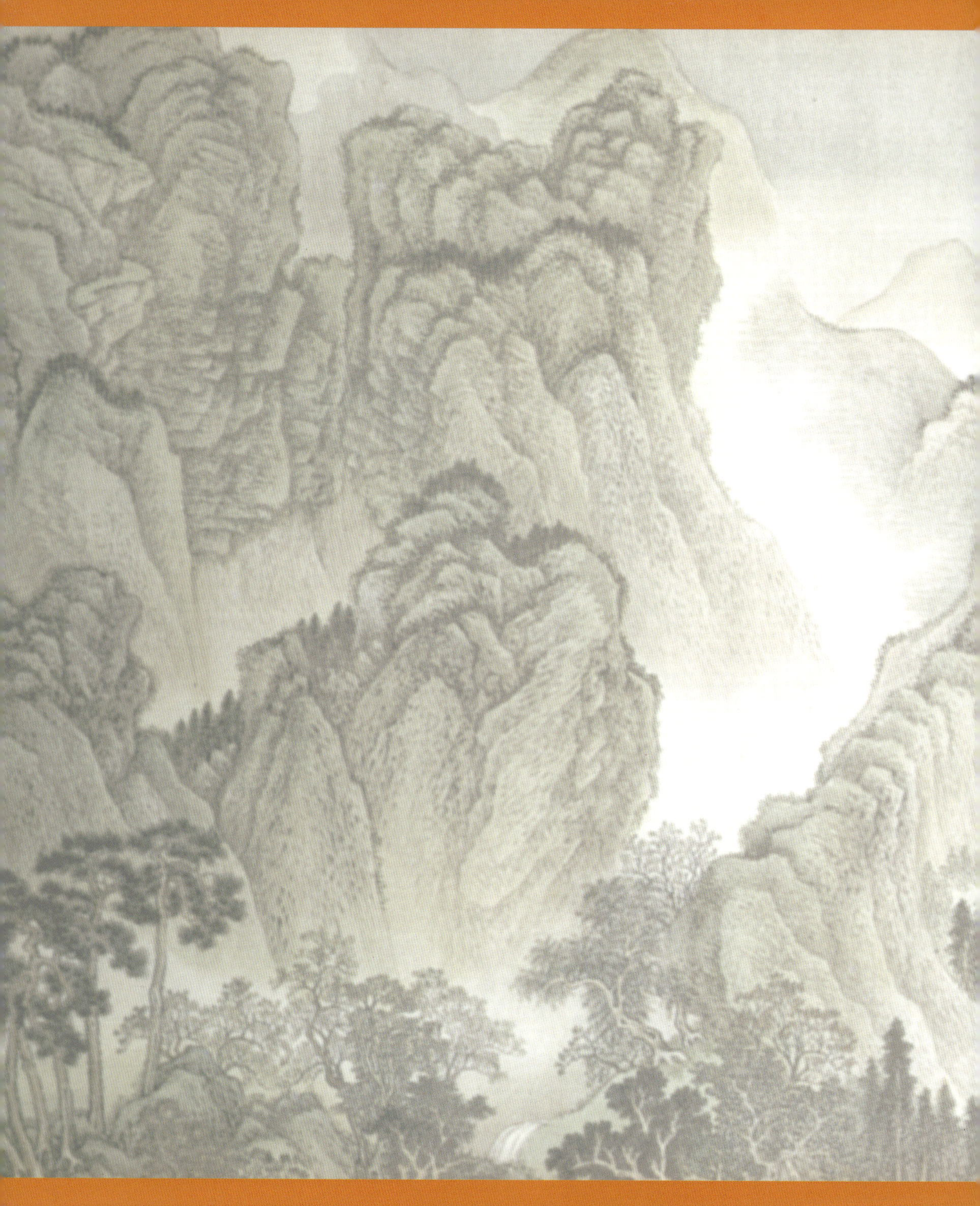

You who dry up
the ocean of psychological poisons
with the blazing fire of wisdom,
You who abide by the Buddha's teaching,
You are a perfect source of liberation.
We pray to you to come here
and be seated amongst us.
We invite you here now
for the sake of all life.
You who open the treasure chest
of the Buddha's teachings for the world,
the Buddha's transmissions
are alive in your hands.

An invocation of the Sixteen Principal Disciples of the Buddha from *The Torch of Precious Jewels* by Jigdral Yeshe Dorje, Dudjom Rinpoche

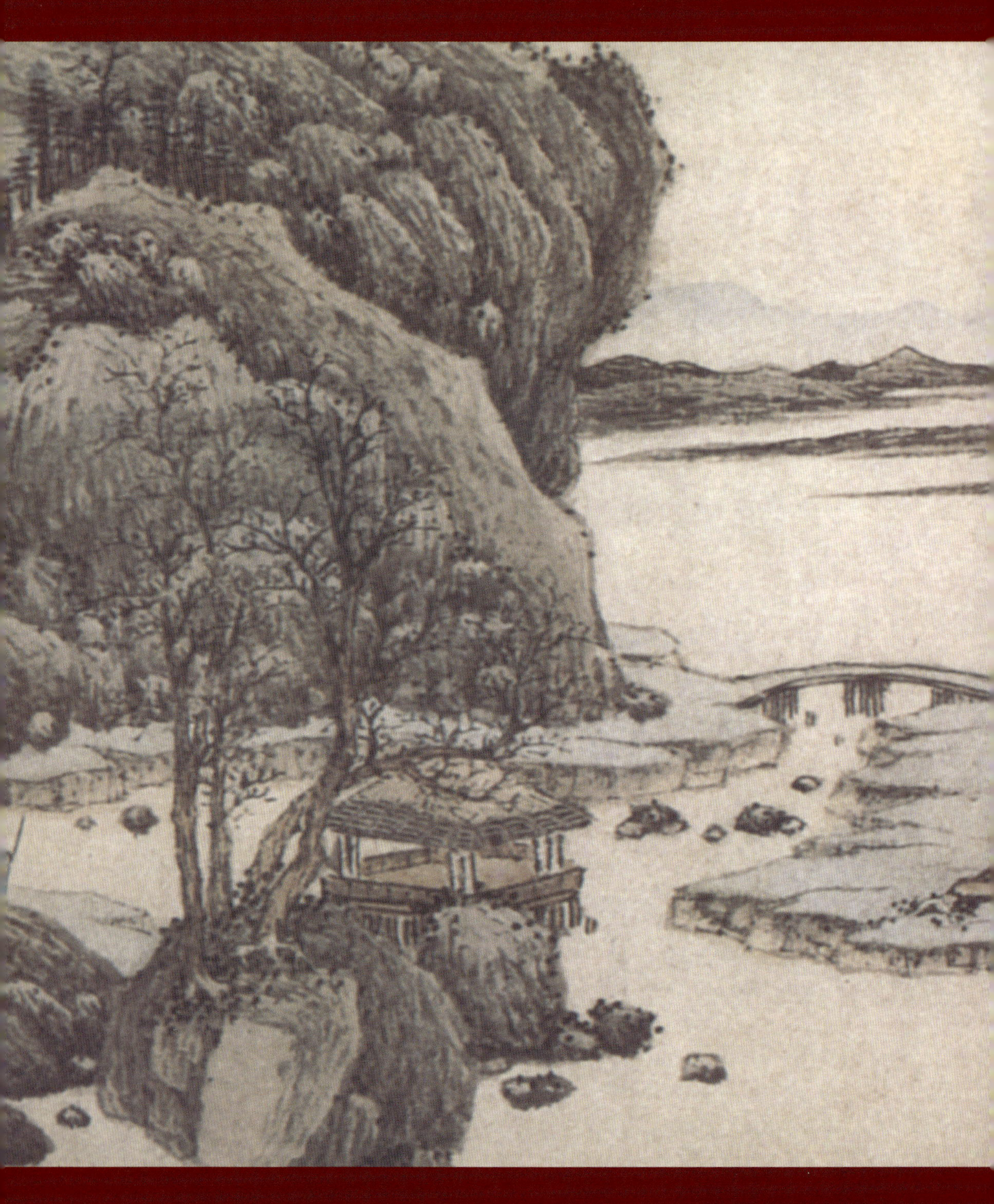

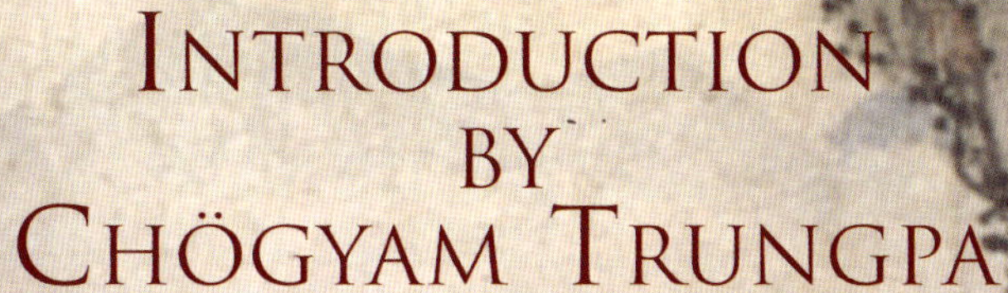

Introduction by Chögyam Trungpa

Interview by Robert Newman
Transcription by Francesca Fremantle
Boulder, Colorado,
August 1974

Many people in America have had striking experiences with these I-Chou Lohan statues but there's limited understanding of what the statues are and how they were made.*

I think we have to look at it very simply. These statues represent, according to the tradition, individuals who had left their homes, and before they left there had been a lot of traumatic experiences of pain and suffering. They then established their relationship with their teacher, in this case the Buddha himself.

The sense of simplicity they experienced in monastic life after being ordained by the Buddha brought a sense of non-verbal experience. I think these statues are expressions of non-verbal experience that the artist had of the state of arhathood. The statues are powerful because they are filled with a state of experience.

**Lohan* is the Chinese translation of the Sanskrit word *arhat*, meaning disciple of the Buddha. It also means a stage or state in the path of meditation.

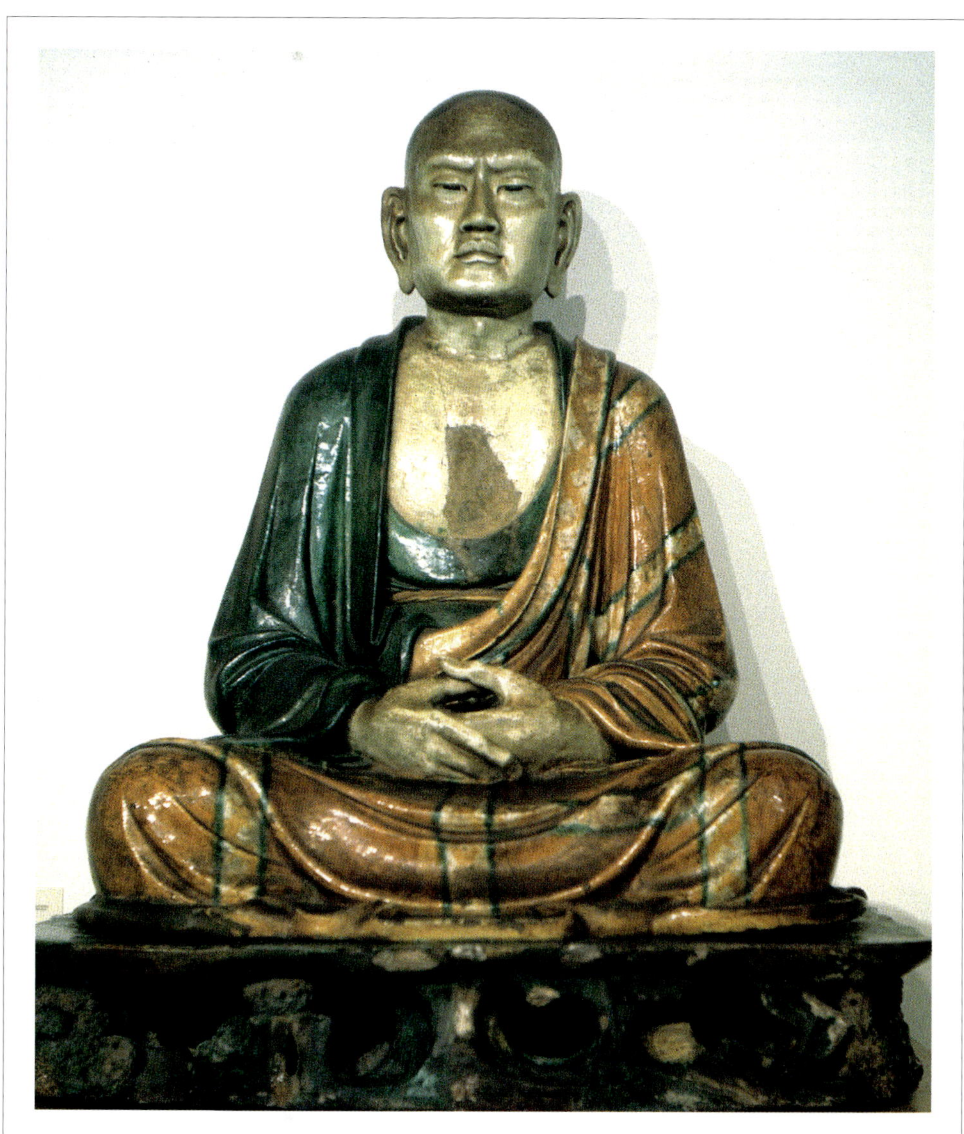

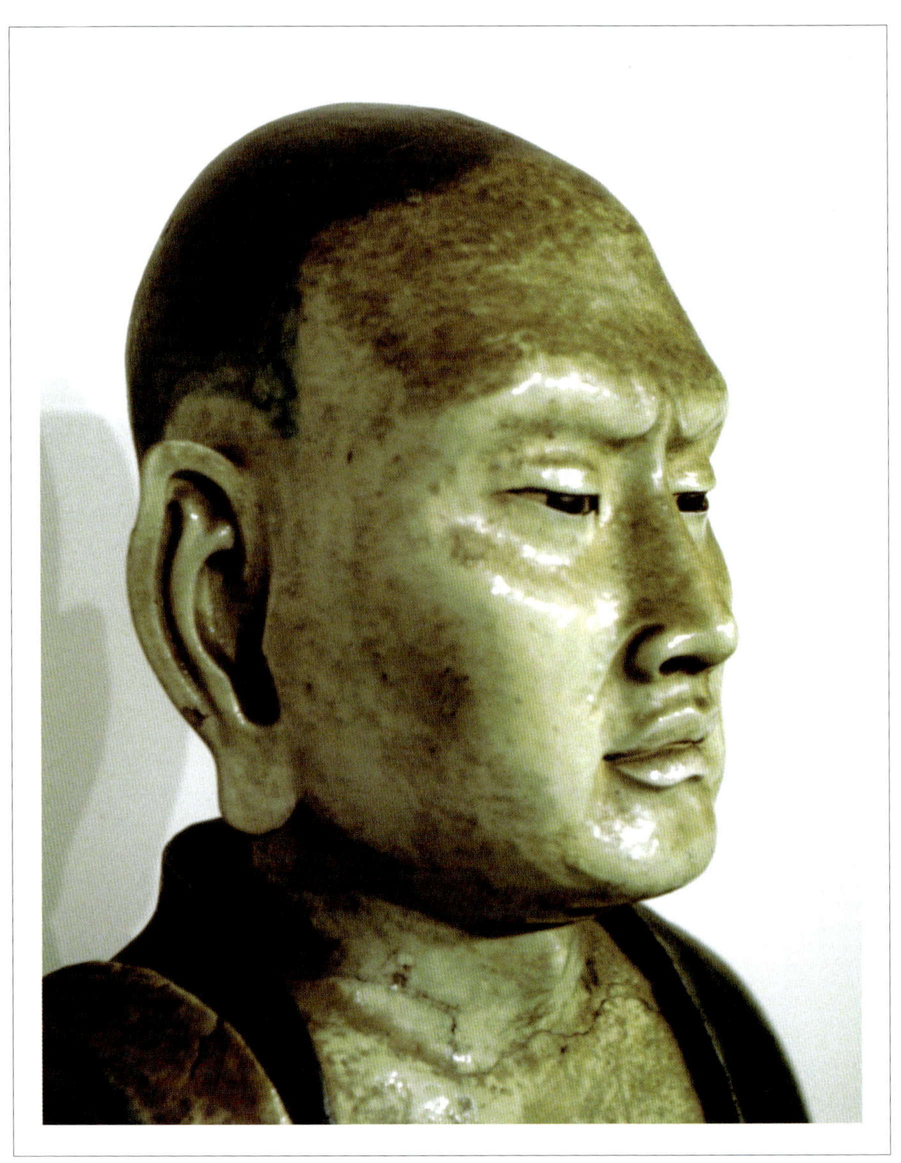

These individuals had left their homes and established themselves in a monastic situation, which in the early days of Buddhism was just living in the jungle or meditating in a cave. They became healthier physically and psychologically. These particular beings represented had that sane living situation and also had the sanity of communication with the Buddha. We could say these images present the particular realization of Buddha's sanity in his direct disciples.

Would you say that these are images of vipashyana meditation?*

I think you could say that the expressions of the statues are very definite. The practice of meditation becomes a day-to-day life situation from the shamatha experience to the vipashyana experience. Therefore many of the postures we see the statues in are very casual ones.

---

*Shamatha-Vipashyana: Shamatha (sanskrit; *shinay*, Tibetan) means "calm abiding," "remaining in quiescence." This is the widely used practice of calming the mind through various concentration techniques, such as following the breath, in order to shift attention from mind to open awareness. From the concentration practices of shamatha, effortless vipashayana meditation naturally arises, a spontaneous "clear seeing," "panoramic awareness." *Vipashyana* is the direct practice of "extraordinary insight."

LOHAN ONE (DETAIL)

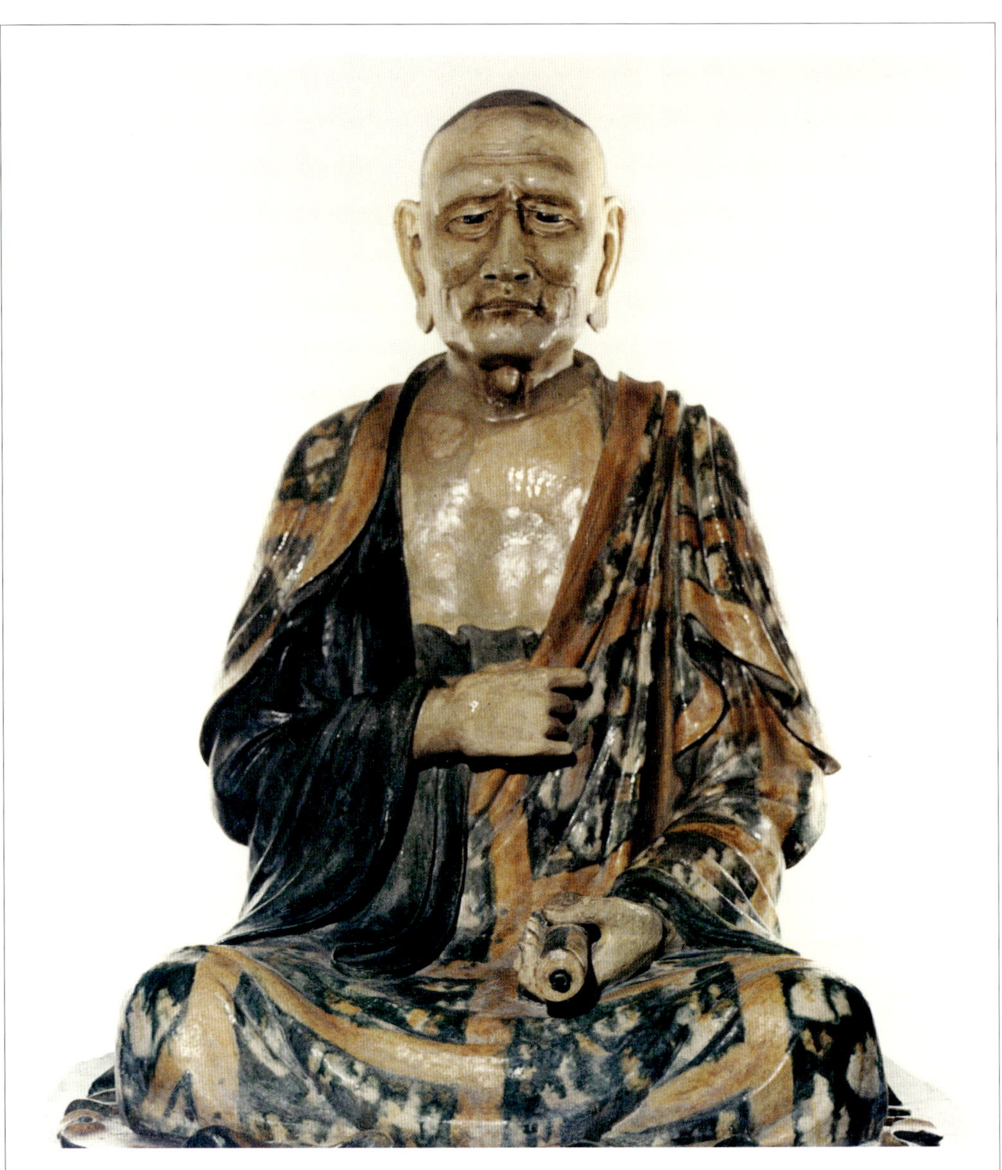

The natural habit of meditation has already been built up and they feel a continuous vipashyana experience. They don't have to pose for it. They have become used to just being that way. These images are actual portraits of how they handle themselves. They also illustrate the particularly Chinese tradition of reverence and respect for teachers. The flowing robes and powerful expressions are comparable to imperial portraits, like a king or monarch who doesn't have to work to improve his subjects. He just handles himself very casually. I would say of the artist that he may have experienced some practice of meditation and some insight. But these images are done with a sense of awe and reverence, in a very sacred application. And so the images are very human and at the same time kind of superhuman.

LOHAN TWO

I think the particularly human quality of the images is most striking to people. The human, life-like qualities create a shock of confrontation in space, something like a mirror. So if the artist was experiencing awe, he was doing so in making extremely human images, faces very related to his own.

I think so. The artist has obviously experienced the living Buddhism that is always present, as well as certain teachers with Buddha-like qualities, so that the Teachings are no myth, but a very real experience. The sense of awe and respect comes together with a sense of ineffableness, an enigmatic quality. The artist would have loved to have experienced that directly, but could only do it by making these portraits. Something is not available to him, but at the same time it is very available to him and almost frightening. A kind of balance takes place. And of course the whole thing is very cultural and hierarchical in approach.

LOHAN TWO (DETAIL)

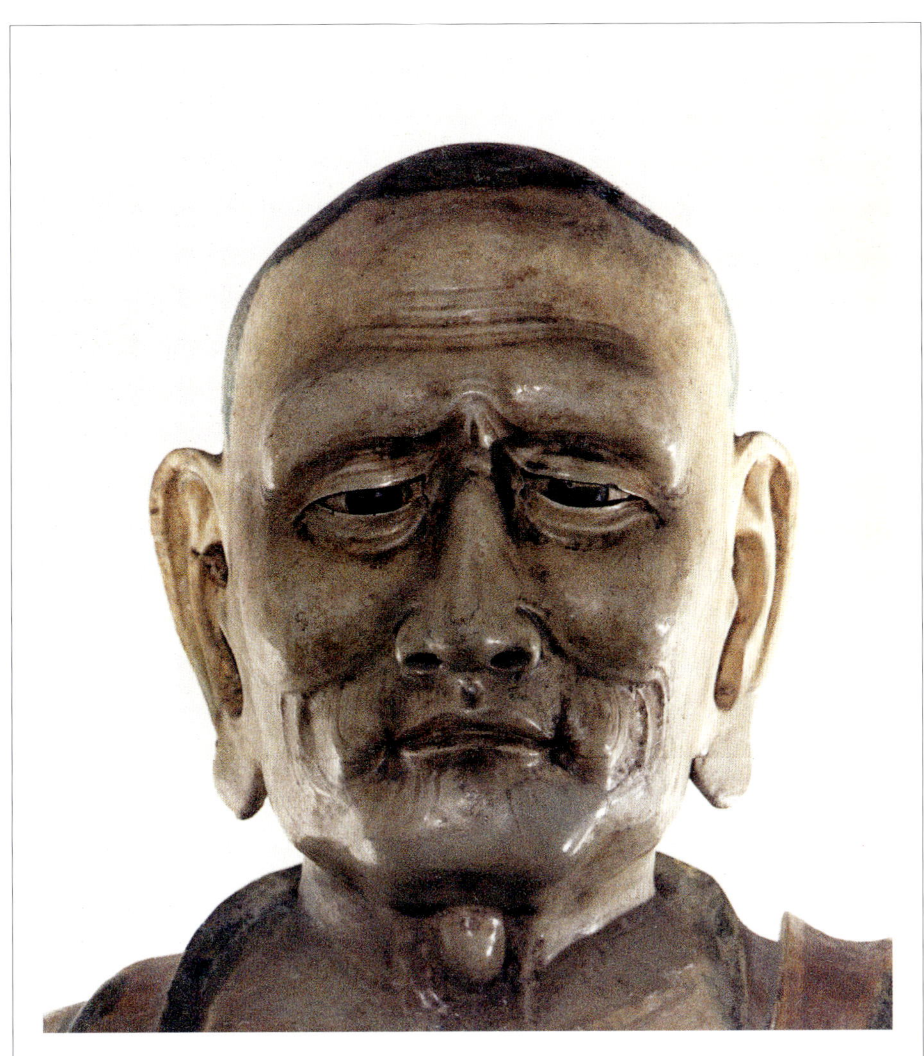

In Indian Buddhism there is less of a hierarchical attitude. Becoming a Buddhist meant transcending the caste system. But when Buddhism entered China, the priest class became very powerful. Buddhism was invited to China by the emperor, the great scholars and the great prime ministers. Traditionally, the abbots are the only people who can put their hands on the emperor's head to bless him. That's known as rajaguru, and such power is never questioned. Even if you question it, there is a sense of mystery. But traditionally that mystery is thrown back in the accomplishments of a person in his life, what he does. The artist achieved what he wanted to achieve.

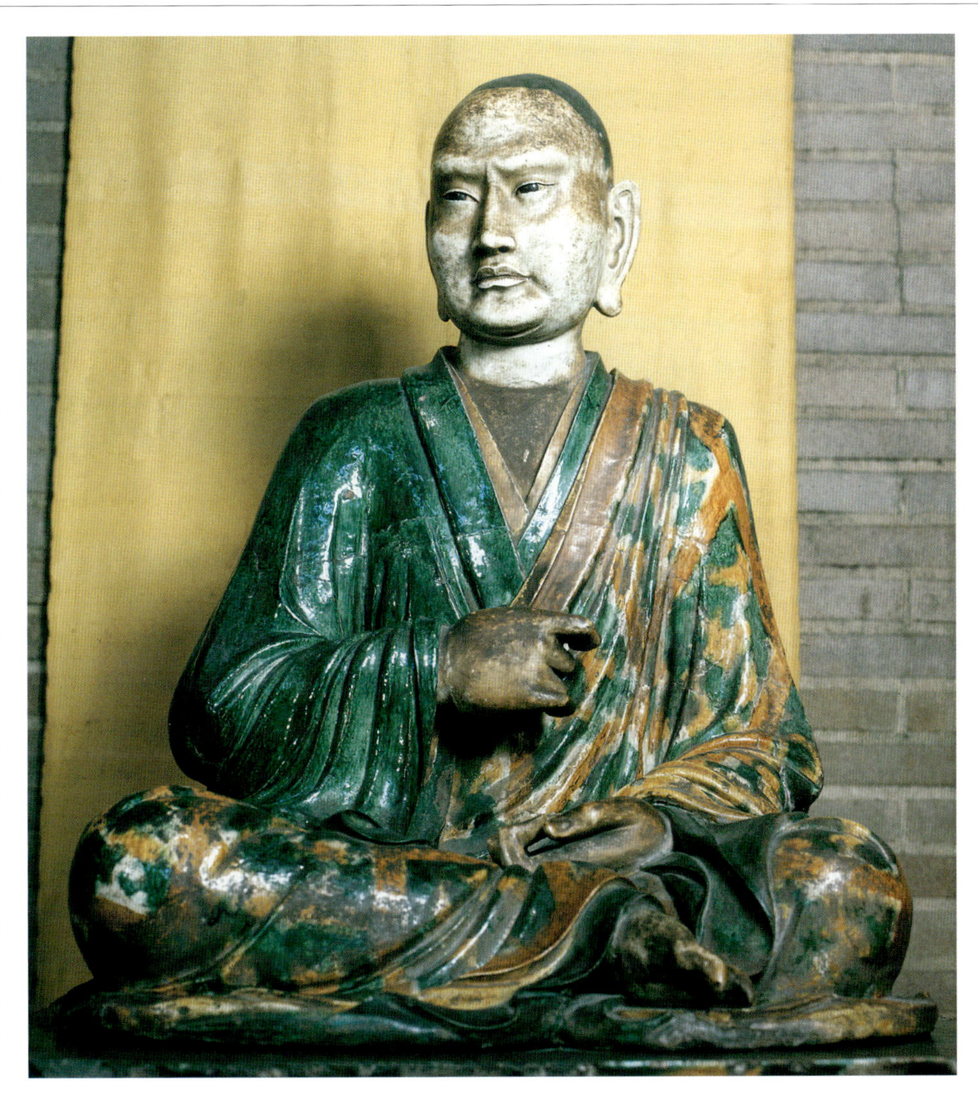

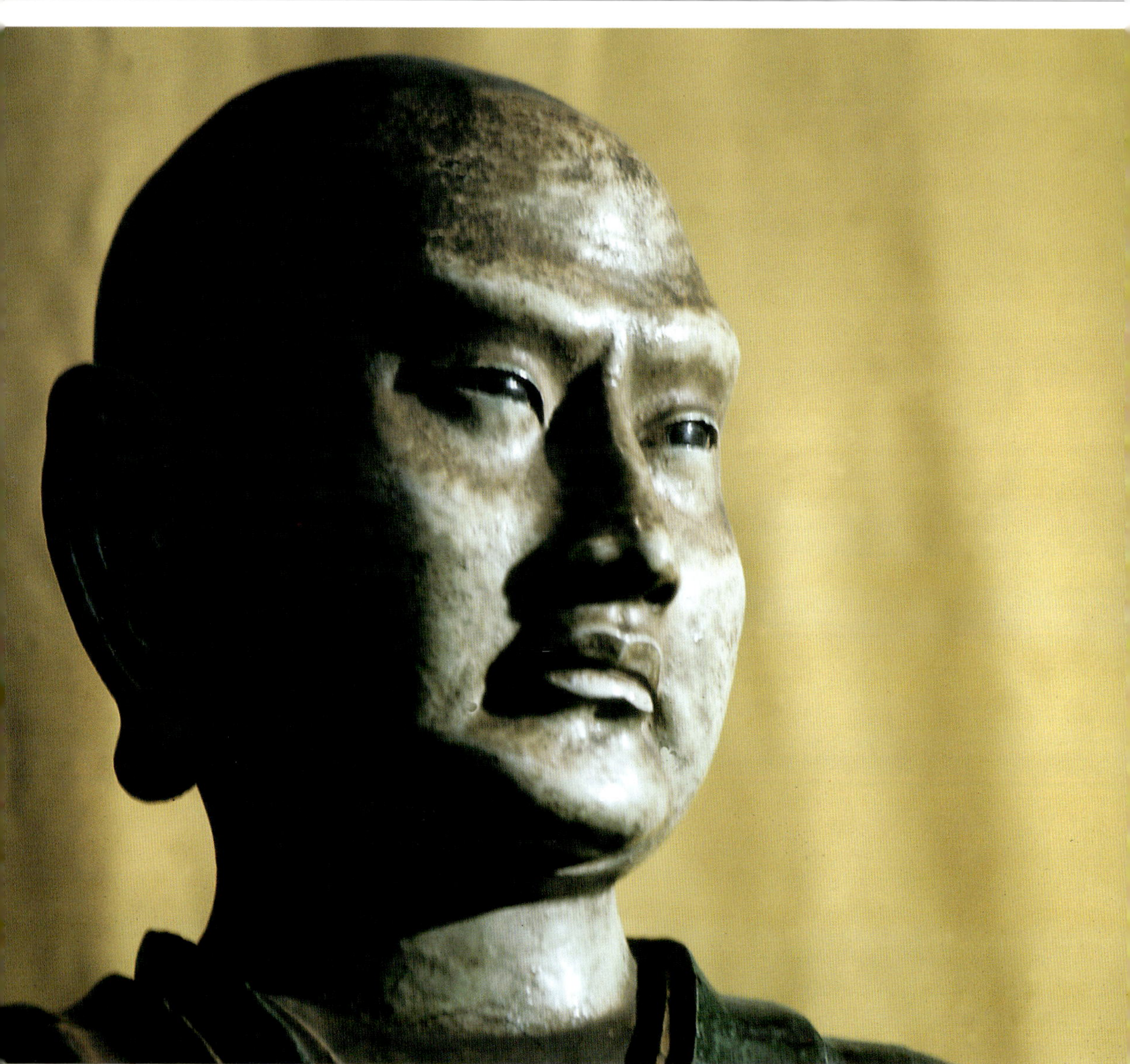

The depiction of sumptuous robes on the Lohans gives them a stately quality while the training they represent calls for simplicity. Do they give the sense of both church power and profound simplicity?

I think so. In the traditional story, the arhats were invited to China by the Emperor, who asked them, 'What can I offer you?' and an arhat answered, "New monastic robes". The Emperor felt that it was a very humble request. He began to measure the bodies of the arhats, and the measuring became completely limitless. In trying to make robes, the whole stock of fabrics in the imperial palace ran out, and he had to tax the local people. He told them to bring not only the traditional yellow and red color cloth, but to bring cloth of any color. So traditionally lohans don't have strictly monastic colors in their clothing. And that comes from a story of the arhats performing a miracle.

LOHAN THREE (DETAIL)

Sets of arhat statues were also made in Tibet, traditionally. They were usually placed in the Shrine of the Sangha. There was a Shrine of the Buddha, which has the biggest buddha statue, usually off the assembly hall. Then there was the Shrine of the Dharma, which contained the Tripitaka books. The Shrine of the Sangha had the arhats and bodhisattvas, particularly the arhats. The hall was huge, and the arhats were set in porcelain caves, made especially to accommodate them.

Yes, like sculptural niches.

Sculptural niches, yes.

Is it true that in Tibet sometimes the disciples were rendered in realistic portraits, like the I-Chou Lohans?

I think that there's a lot of emphasis on the portrait of the guru in the Tibetan tradition of arhat paintings and statues. The same is true of the Eighty-four Siddhas* They usually are depicted like Indian men, with big noses and hair on the chest and unshaven or whatever. There is an element of eccentricity in them.

---

* A siddha (skt) is a man or woman who has developed supernormal powers (siddhis) through meditation realization. The Eighty-four Siddhas were Indian Buddhist masters who can be considered the founders of the siddha lineages that passed into Tibet from the 8th - 11th centuries. The list of the 84 Siddhas as well as details of their lives varies, like the lohan-arhats of China and Tibet. ["Siddha" is also sometimes called "Mahasiddha", Great Siddha.]

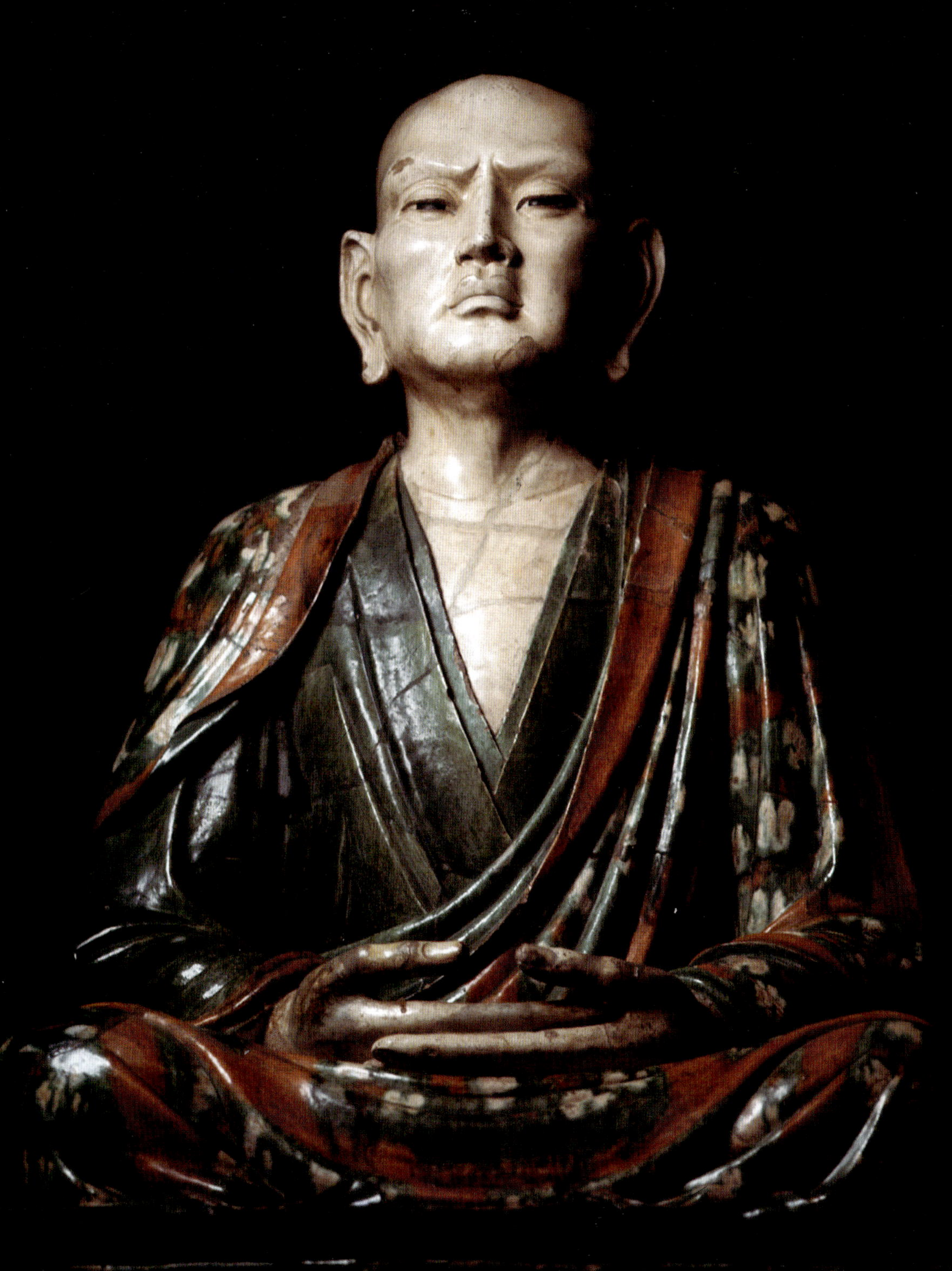

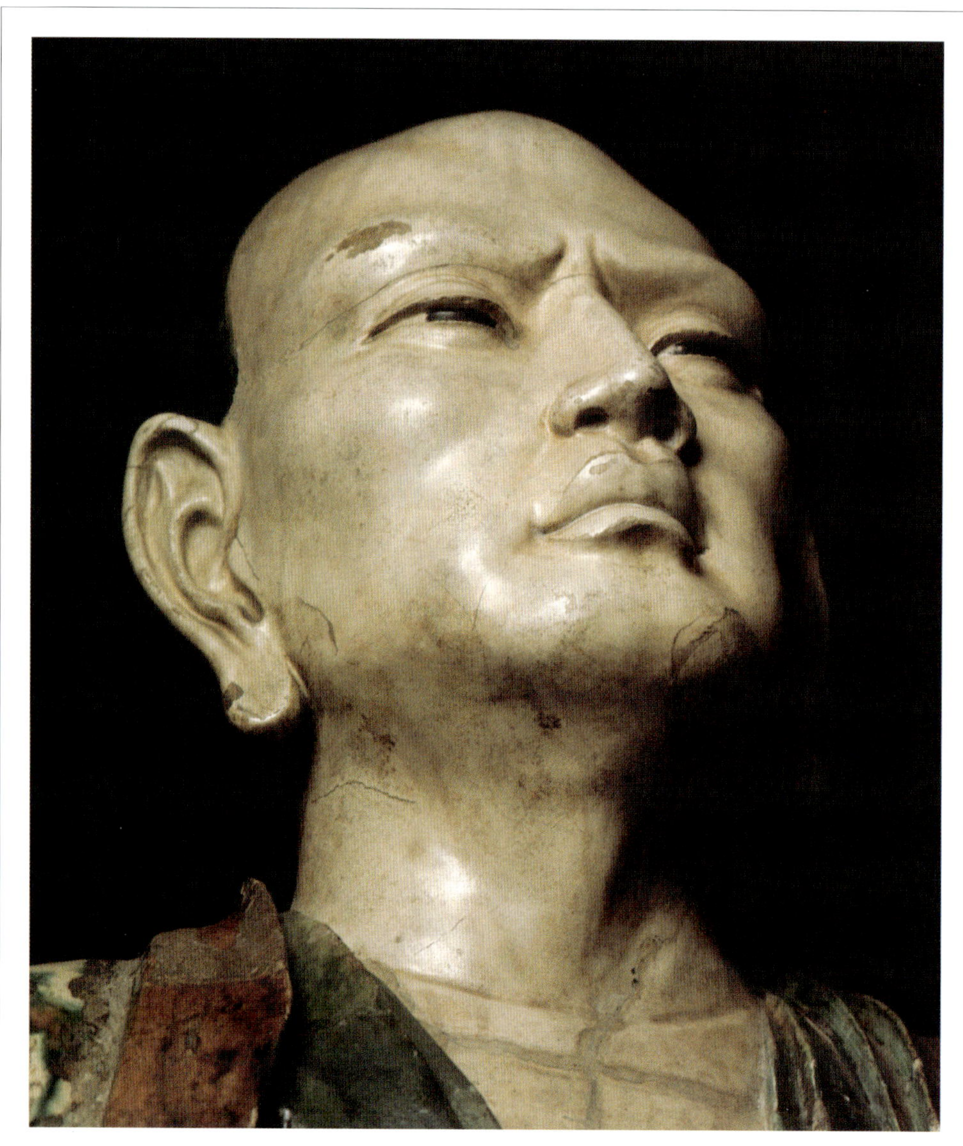

In the Chinese tradition of arhats there are racial mixtures. These I-Chou Lohan statues seem overtly Chinese but there are definitely Aryan features.

Both in China and Tibet the Aryan features are considered somewhat superior. The Buddha had come from Aryan India, and so Aryan also meant somewhat superhuman. The bodhisattvas are much more stylized than the arhats or the Eighty-four Siddhas. The idea in the portrait-like work is that there is a sense of lineage, a sense of personal connection. I think people take delight in a true story, a living person who attained enlightenment. Sometimes it's more refreshing than mythical bodhisattvas or other deities, herukas or dakinis. There's a sense of freshness in the portraits of gurus because the guru is a link between the buddhas, bodhisattvas and herukas and the human world.

LOHAN FOUR (DETAIL)

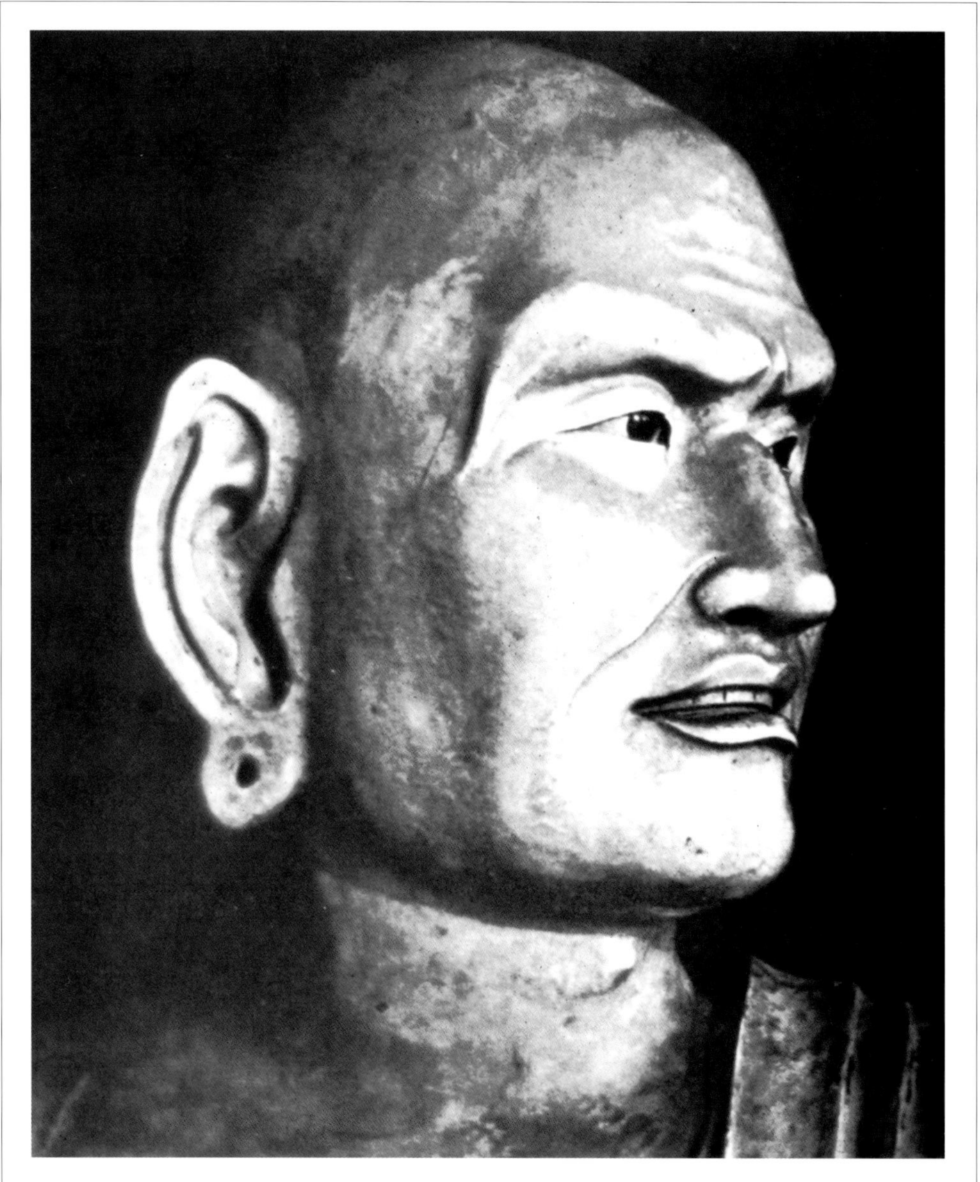

I get the sense that the statues represent a face-to-face situation in the monastery.

I think so. There's a sense of claustrophobia, mirrors mocking your ego. And there's also a sense of simplicity. You can't get away. You can't play games.

The Zen monastic process, you've said, wears down the intellectual mind, almost cuts out intellectual mind, cuts down the ego to allow prajna to function.

Yes, I think that's the point. When we talk about space we aren't talking only of aesthetic space. We're referring to someone's deep loss of ground, which creates real space, real emptiness, and at the same time that brings a sense of dignity and some sense of power.

LOHAN FIVE

Would you consider the I-Chou Lohan statues to be definite representations of initial shunyata realization?

Yes. The situation is that when you've achieved what is known as the arhat state, you've destroyed the enemy, which means you become a conqueror of ego. You've destroyed conflicting emotions, which automatically brings the sense of shunyata. The arhat experience is the prajna, the sword, which cuts through ego, bringing the experience of shunyata. There's a definite link with becoming a warrior.

Aren't conquering self and making friends with oneself interrelated? Doesn't the process contain self-exposure?

Conquering obstacles of ego is not so much a relief as gaining a new sense of power, a new sense of openness, which brings an all-seeing quality. What is known as mahavipashyana experience automatically becomes the vanguard of prajna experience. The presentation of arhats or lohans here is like a sword with an ornamental handle and guard. However, the sword blade is very naked. I would say that the lohans' realization is perhaps at the level of the First Bhumi, the Bhumi of Joy. And I think that, from there onwards, some of the mahasiddhas would be the images of further realization. There's a little

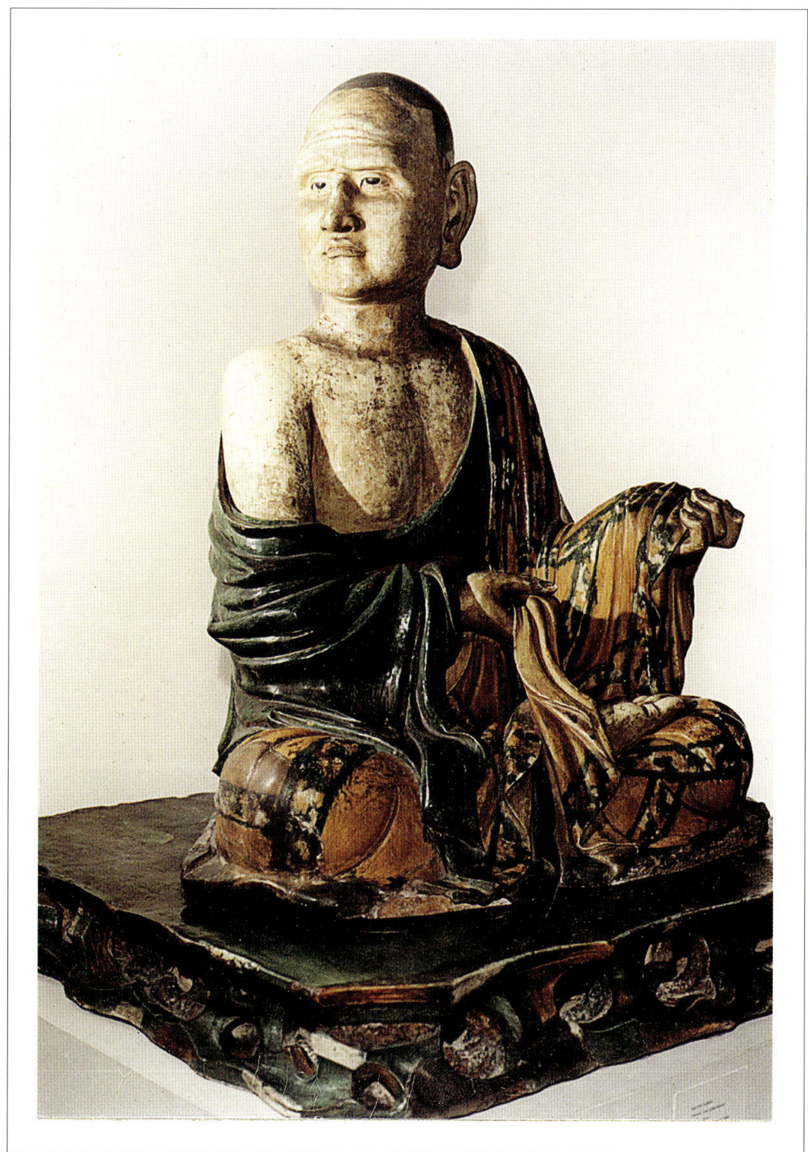

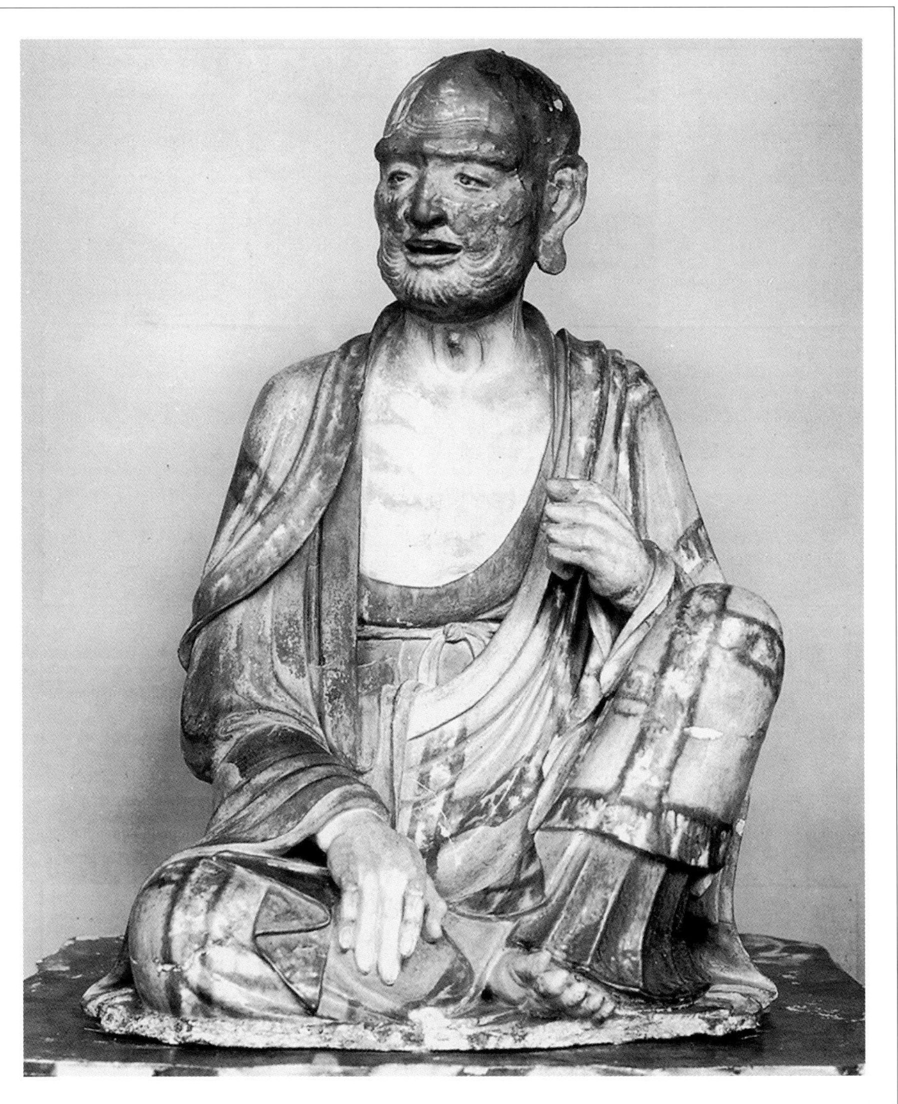

22

craziness in the mahasiddha iconography, as there is in this arhat energy. The craziness is there from the First Bhumi onwards to the Vajrayana, which is another development of the iconography.

Could you speak of these lohans in terms of the Four Noble Truths?

I think these statues embody the whole thing, the Four Noble Truths. There is a sense of being on the path and a sense of experiencing the cessation of suffering. Knowing the Four Noble Truths simultaneously depends on seeing from all viewpoints. I think the artist achieved this work of art because he's true to himself. He just executed it as simply and as impressively as possible, from his own experience of the practice of meditation.

LOHAN SEVEN

Do you know of any other works of Chinese art that represent higher Mahayana meditation? If this is the level of the First Bhumi, can you think of any Chinese Buddhist works of art that represent a higher degree of realization?

Well, there's one of the kinds of bodhisattva statues that have expressions of compassion and gentleness, but with immovability and solidness. The bodhisattva images are highly ornamented and less monastic. They have a less contemplative expression. There's more of a kind of inquisitiveness of how to conduct compassion toward a person. An interesting point about the Chinese expression of the bodhisattvas is that they often have Chinese facial structure, bone structure, but at the same time the costume is always Indian. In Tibet, there were eight bodhisattva sculptures carved in a giant rock that was close to my monastery. They were dressed in imperial costumes, actually wearing imperial hats. Eight ancient emperors. The bodhisattvas become interesting.

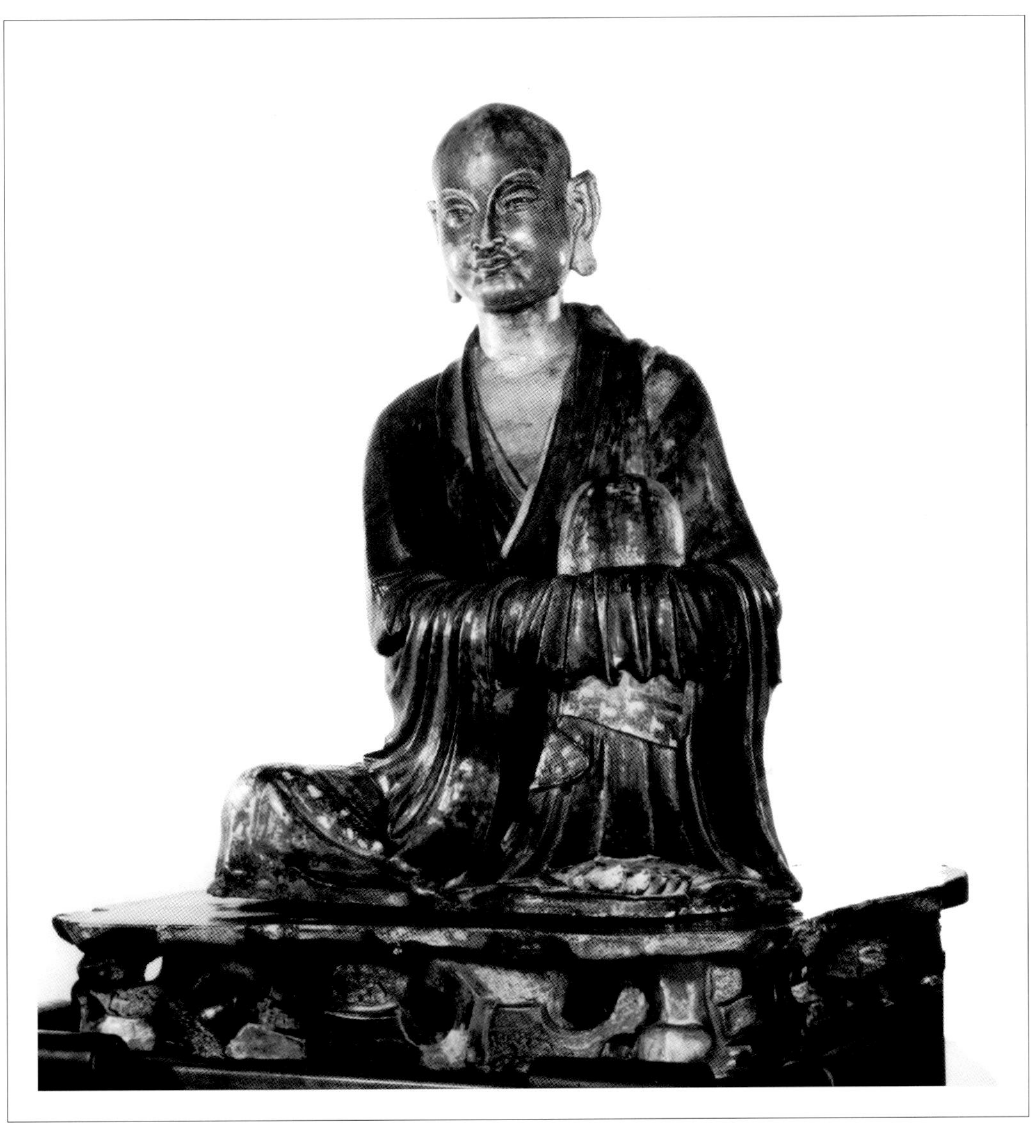

But I think that if a person would really like to work traditionally with the Teachings, this lohan imagery should be studied first. First completely understand the arhat sculptures or the principle of the sculptures. Then, after that, probably comes a glimpse of how bodhisattvas work. And then there are the various Tantric deities in Tibet and Japan. There's a continuity in all this.

Maybe one last question, about the stillness quality of the Lohans. Are the statues expressive of stillness?

I think the sense of stillness comes from the sense of solidness. Although these statues are iconographically informed, with heads turned or holding robes, at the same time there's a sense of definite solidness, a sense of immobility. If you see a blade of grass, it's not an image of solidness, because at any moment it can be flickered by wind. But there are statues that have a sense of dignity and power that present a great sense of sanity, of immovability. It could be a very small statue or it could be a big one, and it could have that quality.

LOHAN FOUR (DETAIL)

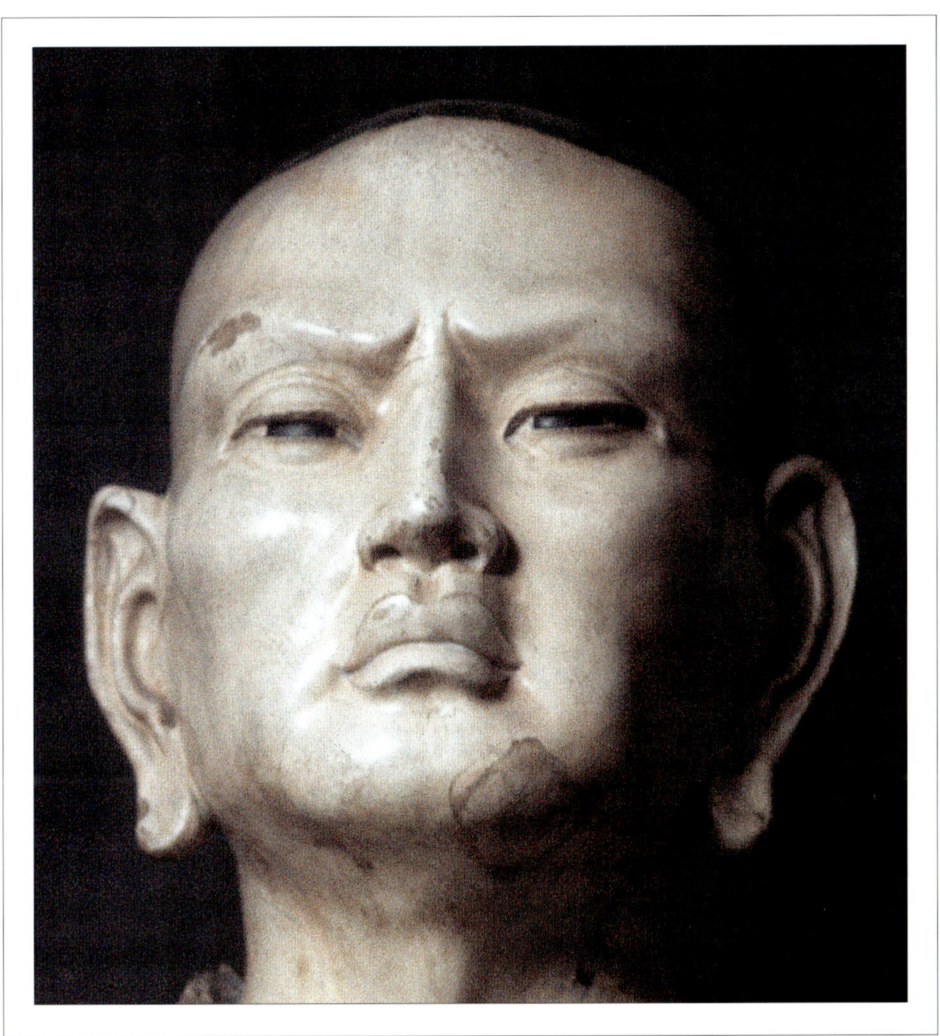

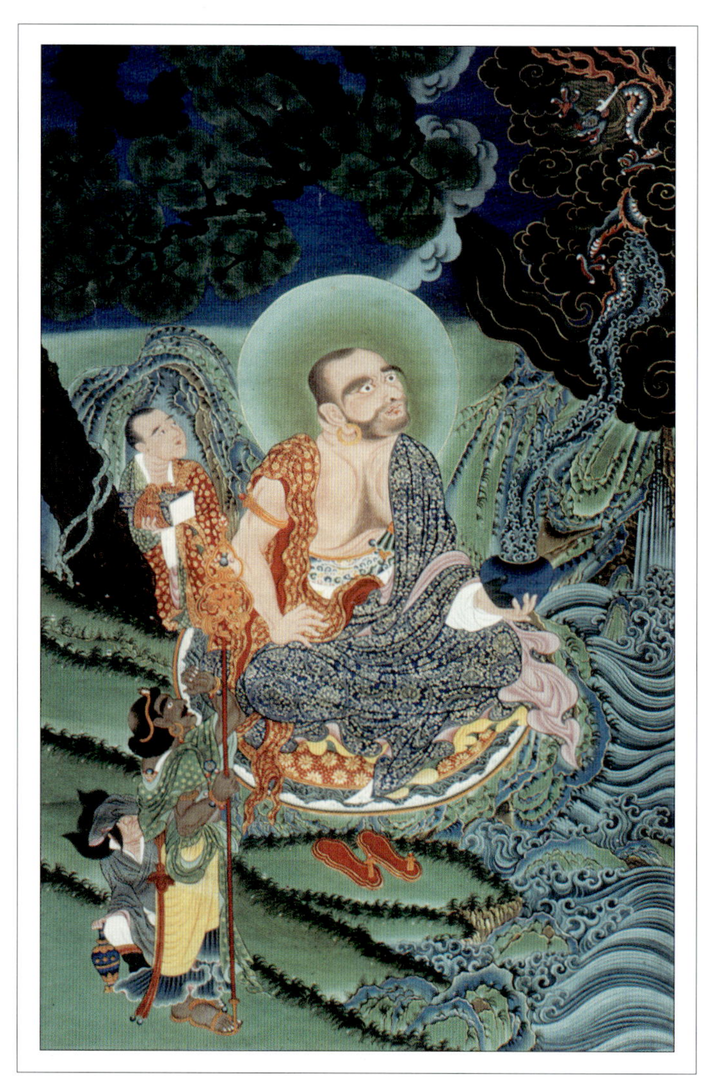

Arhat Nagasena, Bhutanese Thangka

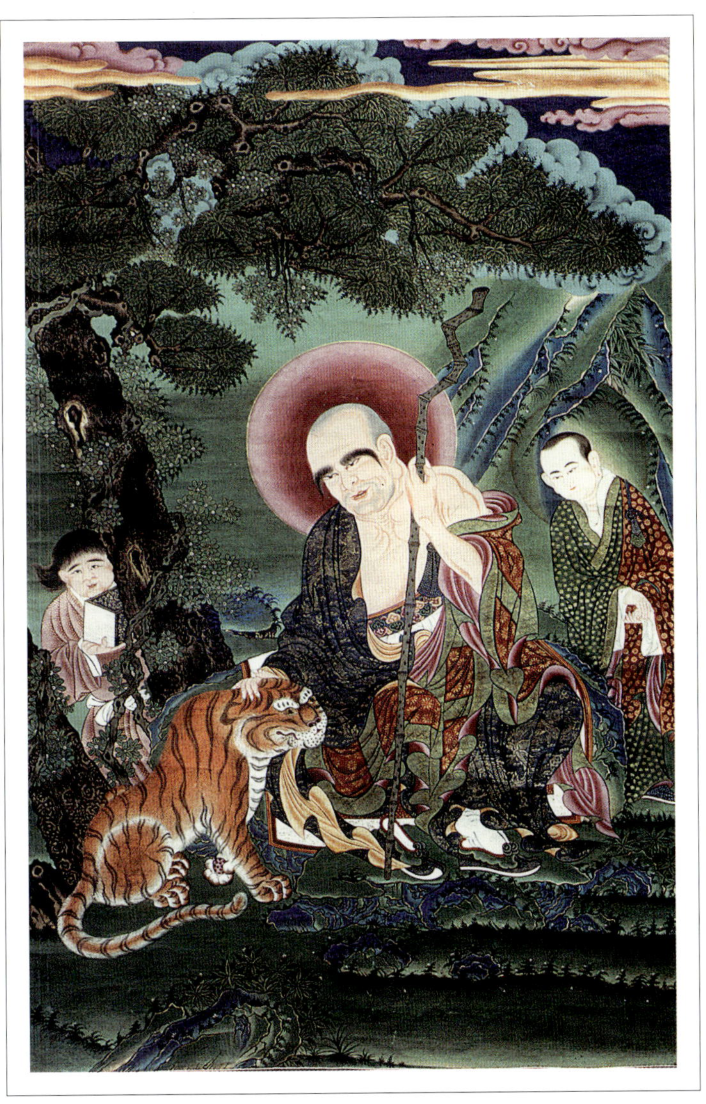

Arhat Dharmatala, Bhutanese Thangka

Living Images Of Meditation

Several ceramic statues of Lohans, legendary disciples of Shakyamuni Buddha, were brought into the Peking art market in 1913. They had been found by pirates in a secluded shrine cave, high on a mountain, not easily accessible, near I-Chou, Hopei Province. The statues may have been in the cave for centuries.[1] They are called the "I-Chou Lohans." All are distinguished by a dramatic life-like presence. We do not know who made the statues or where they were made. There were probably 16 or 18 in the original set. They may have been made in a ceramic factory or in a monastery. We will never know the external circumstances of their creation and yet these disciples look as fresh and alive as if they just came out of the kiln. We can sense from them the depth and range of the entire original work.

1. A commemorative tablet in the cave where the statues had been safeguarded indicated that they had "come from far away." Other indications are that they were stored in the cave when a nearby monastery was dismantled. High on a mountain, and difficult to access, some statues may have been destroyed and some damaged in the ascent and descent from the shrine cave.

Lohan One

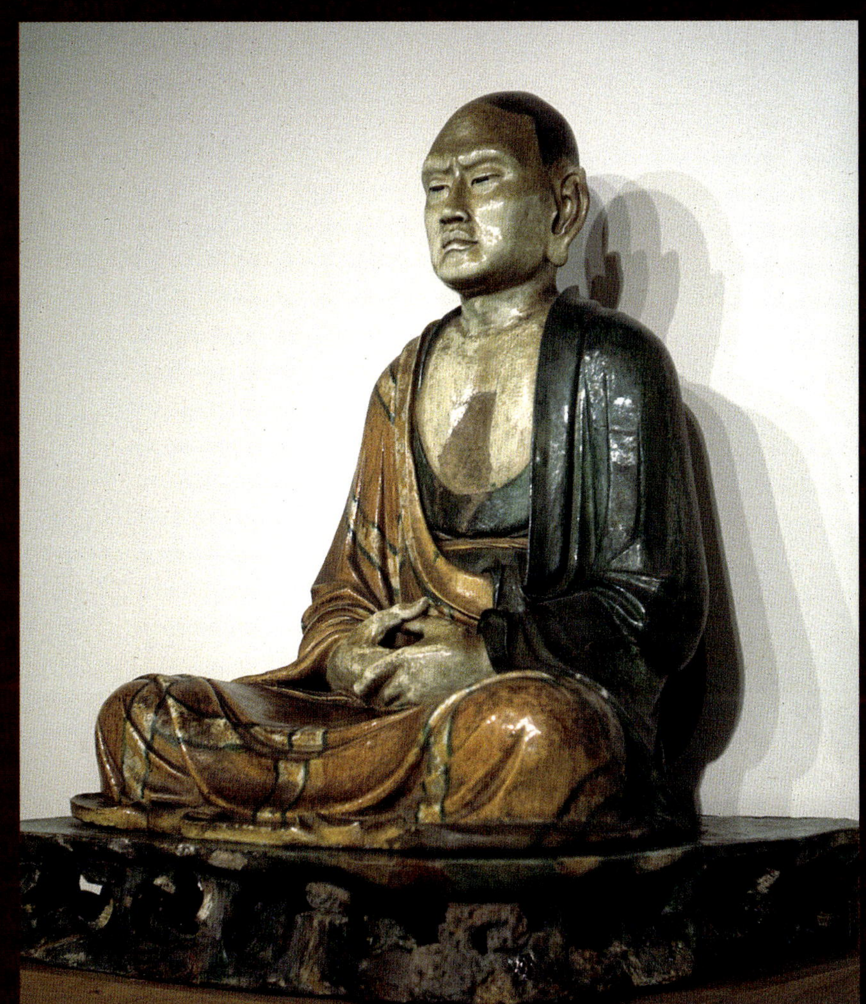

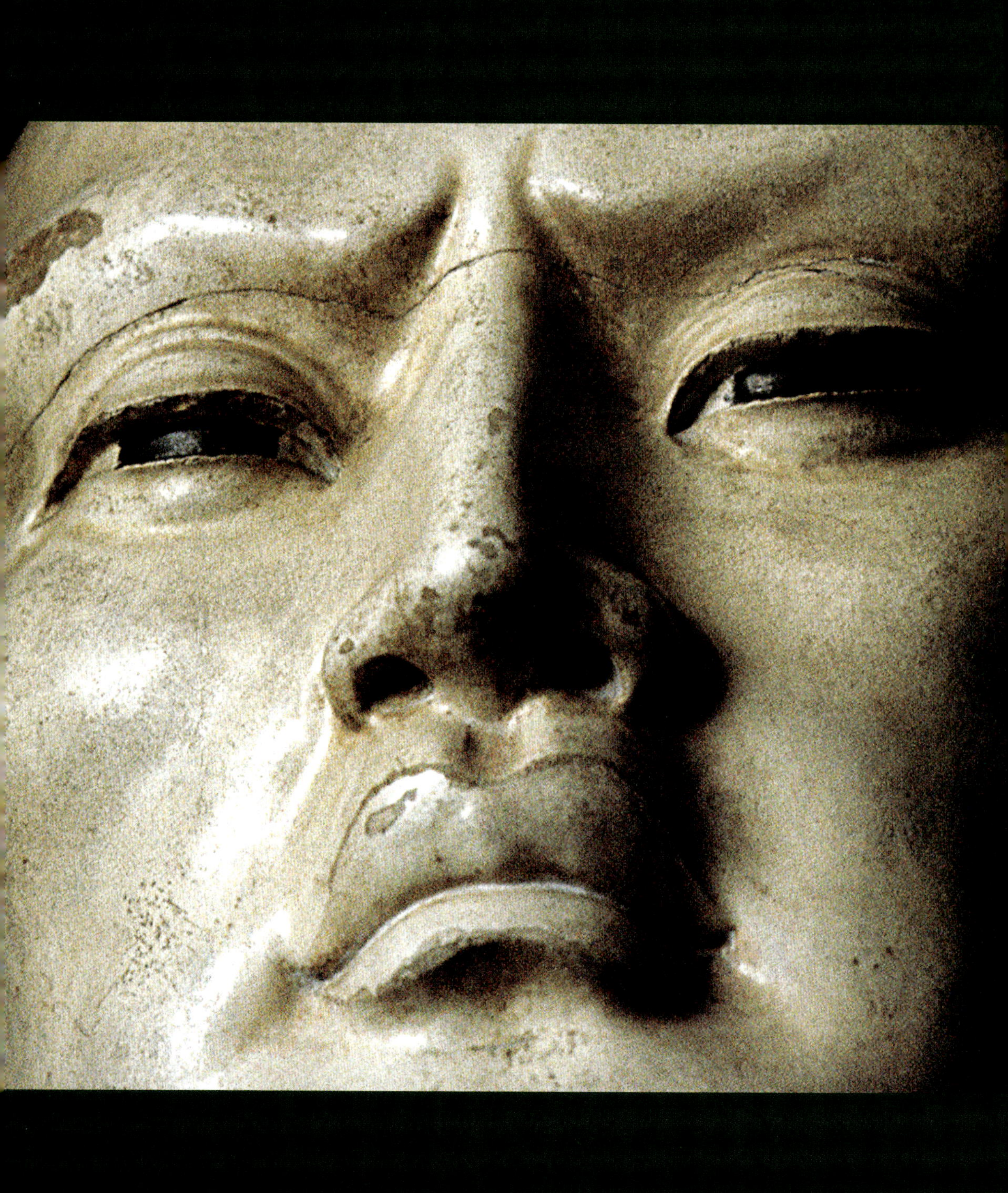

The original set of statues was a large-scale work representing direct connection to the Buddha. The statues are human images with superhuman features. They are living portraits of meditation that connect us to our potential, the awakened state.

Fredrick Perzynski remembers when the first of the I-Chou Lohan statues appeared in the Peking art market: "At the time we called him a priest since, despite his traditionally elongated ears, he emanated the striking pictorial power of a portrait." Upon discovering another of the I-Chou Lohans, he notes: "His neck is broken off, as well as a piece from his shoulder and his feet. In his hands he holds a scroll. His head leans against the wall next to the torso. In its coloring of faded ivory it appears like the head of a decapitated man. As on the previous occasions in seeing [I-Chou Lohan statues] its powerful expression affects me like an electric shock."[2]

---

[2] See Marion Wolfe's article, "The Lohans From I-Chou"; Oriental Art, Vol. XV, #1, Spring 1969. Perzynski's involvement in the discovery of the I-Chou Lohans is described there. He seems to have been centrally responsible for the placement of several of the I-Chou Lohans in western museums. The one he described above is LOHAN TWO.

Sometime in 1969, I was wandering through the Metropolitan Museum of Art in New York City. I walked into the presence of two of the I-Chou Lohan statues. At the moment that I started to step closer to one of them (LOHAN TWO), I had what is the most remarkable experience I've ever had with a work of art. I saw something impossible, something miraculous. The statue was alive. I thought what I was seeing was a living form. I was then moved by the sense of flesh, the tissue quality in the throat, in the mouth, up into the cheekbones, into the enlarged brows, over and between the eyes. The statue had large buddha ears. The mouth was closed and the expression was silent. The eyes were open and I felt that they were seeing me. There seemed to be a force in the eyes, and knowledge of flesh and mind, a real sense of the world, a haunting smile, and stillness. I began to ask about the statues. People thought they were extraordinary, and some had striking experiences with them, seeing them as alive.

Coomaraswamy[3] on Aesthetic Shock: "The Pali word *samvega* is often used to denote the shock or wonder

---

[3] Coomaraswamy, A.D. *Figures of Speech, Figures of Thought.* London (Luzak and Co., 1946), p.205.

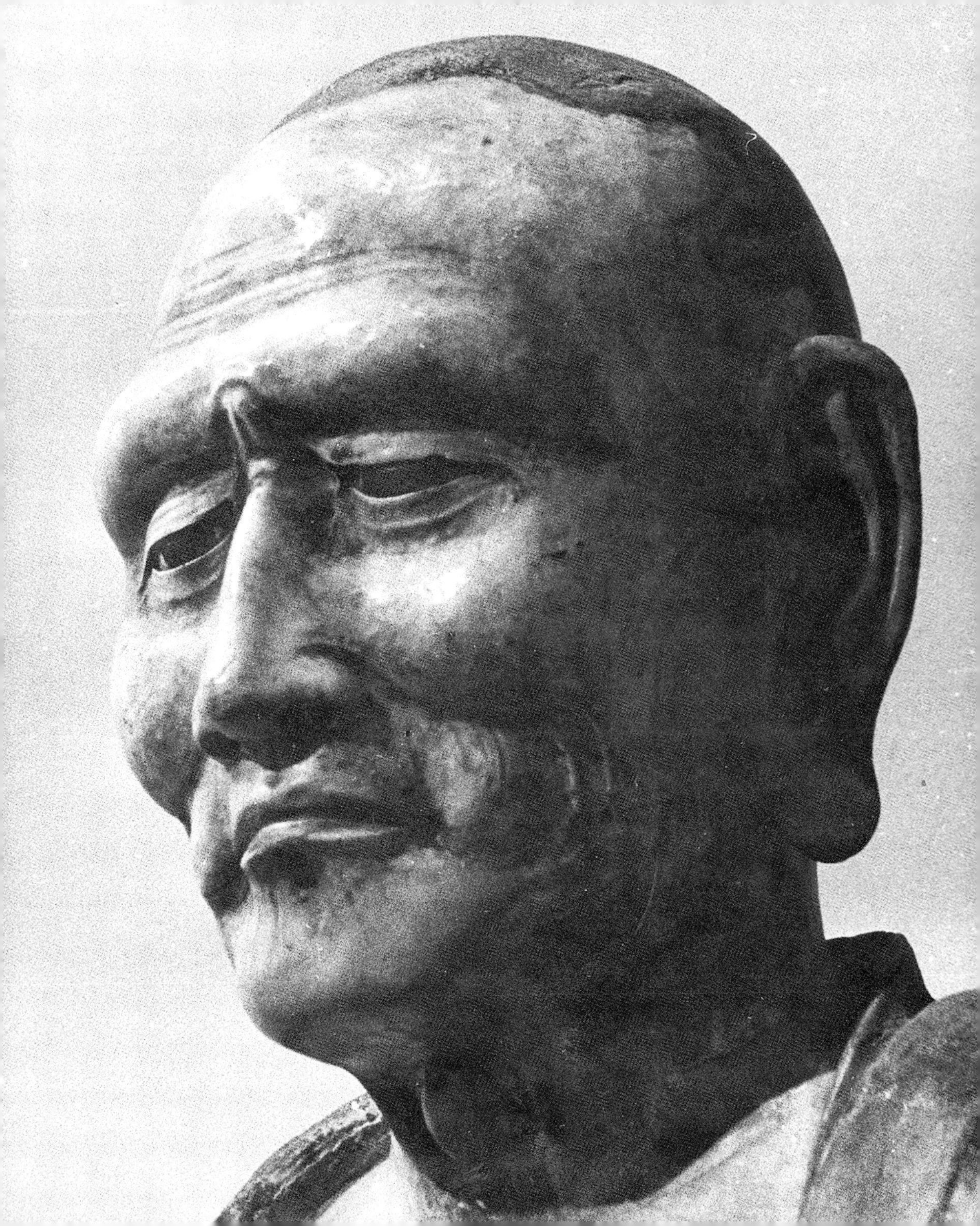

that may be felt when the perception of a work of art becomes a serious experience... the "shock" or "thrill" need not involve a recoil but may be one of supersensual delight. For example, the cultivation of the Seven Factors of Awakening (to truth) accompanied by the notion of the Arrest (of the vicious causes of all pathological conditions) of which the seventh [Factor of Awakening] is an Impartiality (upekha)...because it cannot be told and does not appear."[3]

The word *Buddha* means fully awakened one. The statues are images of lives devoted to meditation, devoted to awakening. They are images of the resting of intention, the resting of grasping and fixation, to be free of movement, seeing with compassion. The statues give us contact with a state beyond mind, a state of experience beyond words.

The Disciples carry the transmissions from the Buddha Shakyamuni. They open the treasure and give full blessings of the Buddha. They are as essential to the foundations of Buddhism as the Apostles are to Christianity.

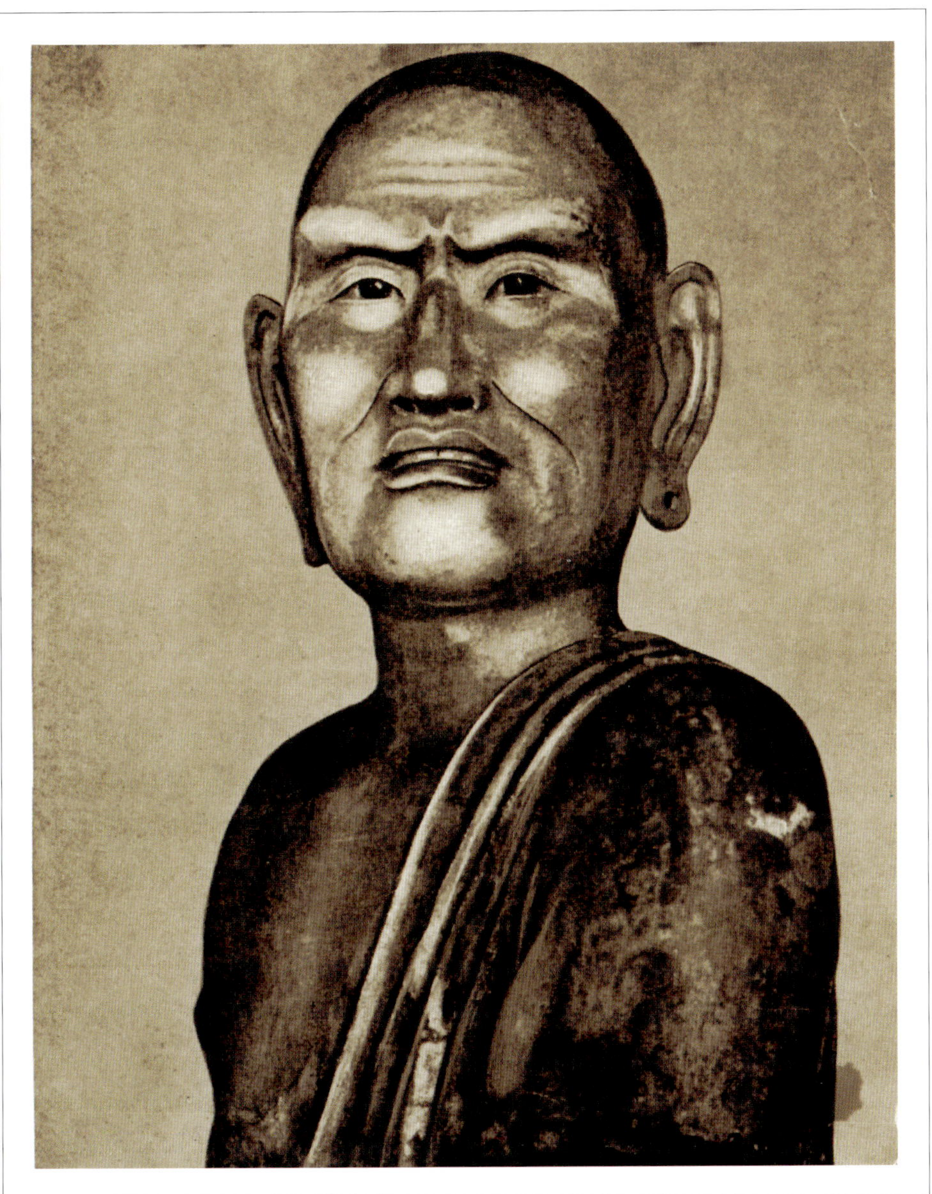

The Disciples and the imagery of meditation were inspirations for the art of many Buddhist countries.

R. I. Hobson[4] on the LOHAN ONE:
"The quatrefoil ornament on the bands of the robes...The clay tougher than in the tomb figures...The Lohan modelled with a free hand, showing in every detail the loving touch of a master...The Lohan represents an art which is intelligible in all lands and in all ages. Its simplicity and grandeur give it an irresistible appeal...The 'life movement' in the figure is a keynote of T'ang art and applies equally to life in motion and life in repose. The Lohan is revelation of the greatness of Chinese sculpture in its classic period and it may fairly claim a place among the masterpieces of all time... Regarded only from the potter's standpoint, it was no small achievement to have built up and fired such a mass of plastic clay without shrinkage or loss of form. Such triumphs are rare because of the great difficulty in their manufacture; but once accomplished, they have an advantage over sculpture in other materials, because the soft clay responds so readily to the touch of the artist's fingers and the rich, warm glazes clothe it with colors which do not fade."

---

4 Hobson, R.L., *A New Chinese Masterpiece at the British Museum.* The Burlington Magazine, vol. XXV, no. 5, 1914, p.262.

Dr. Otto Kummel on LOHAN FIVE:
"...never has East Asian sculpture imparted a more grandiose, immediately recognizable form to the passionate struggle for spiritual enlightenment which is expressed in the Arhat, in contrast to the Buddhas and Boddhisattvas." [5]

Peter Swann on the I-Chou Lohans:
"...technically they are masterpieces, artistically they have an immediate personal impact. Religiously they reflect a belief in an all-embracing salvation." [6]

Marion Wolfe on the I-Chou Lohans:
"Even a generation accustomed to comparatively abstract modes of expression cannot but respond in awe to these consumately styled potrayals of human spirituality."[7]

Michael Sullivan:
*"These figures are not so much portraits of individual monks, as expressions of a variety of spiritual states. In the face of the young arhat (*LOHAN FOUR*) is portrayed all the inward struggle, the intensity of concentration, of the meditative sects of which Chan was the chief. When we turn to* LOHAN TWO, *we*

---

[5] Dr. Otto Kummel, *Die Ausstellung der Saminlong Perzynski in Berliner Kunstgewerke Museum, Ostasiatische Zeitschrift*, II, pp 457-61.
[6] Peter Swann, *Literature of China, Korea and Japan*, Fredrick Praeger, NY, 1963, pp 125, 143.
[7] Marion Wolfe, as above, pp 57

see in the bony skull lined features and deep-set eyes of an old man. The outcome of that struggle; it has taken its toll of the flesh, but the spirit has emerged serene and triumphant"[8]

Jessica Rawson on the I-chou Lohans:
"In China, a tradition of sixteen louhans was known from the fifth century AD, and by the Tang period they were often depicted in groups of eighteen.... As a tribute to their humanity in the transmission of Buddhist teaching, they were often shown with strongly characterized faces, as if they were particularly recognizable individuals...(re: LOHAN ONE:) A stern but serene face gives the impression of an individual but at the same time suggests a commanding religious belief, embracing all upon whom his gaze falls... such images were not intended as depictions of individuals; the impression was created of a particular person in order to fulfill a religious purpose, in this case to promote the view that all mankind might aspire to the spiritual understanding represented by the luohan."[9]

The statues appear to have been made by one master artist, probably with assistants to help with the arduous kneading and building up of the clay and to help with the kiln firing process. All this might have been done in a public ceramic facility or a Buddhist building.

---

8 Michael Sullivan, *The Arts of China*, p 154-5
University of California Press, Ltd., London, England, 1979

9 Rawson, Jessica, *The British Museum Book of Chinese Art*, 1993, p. 157

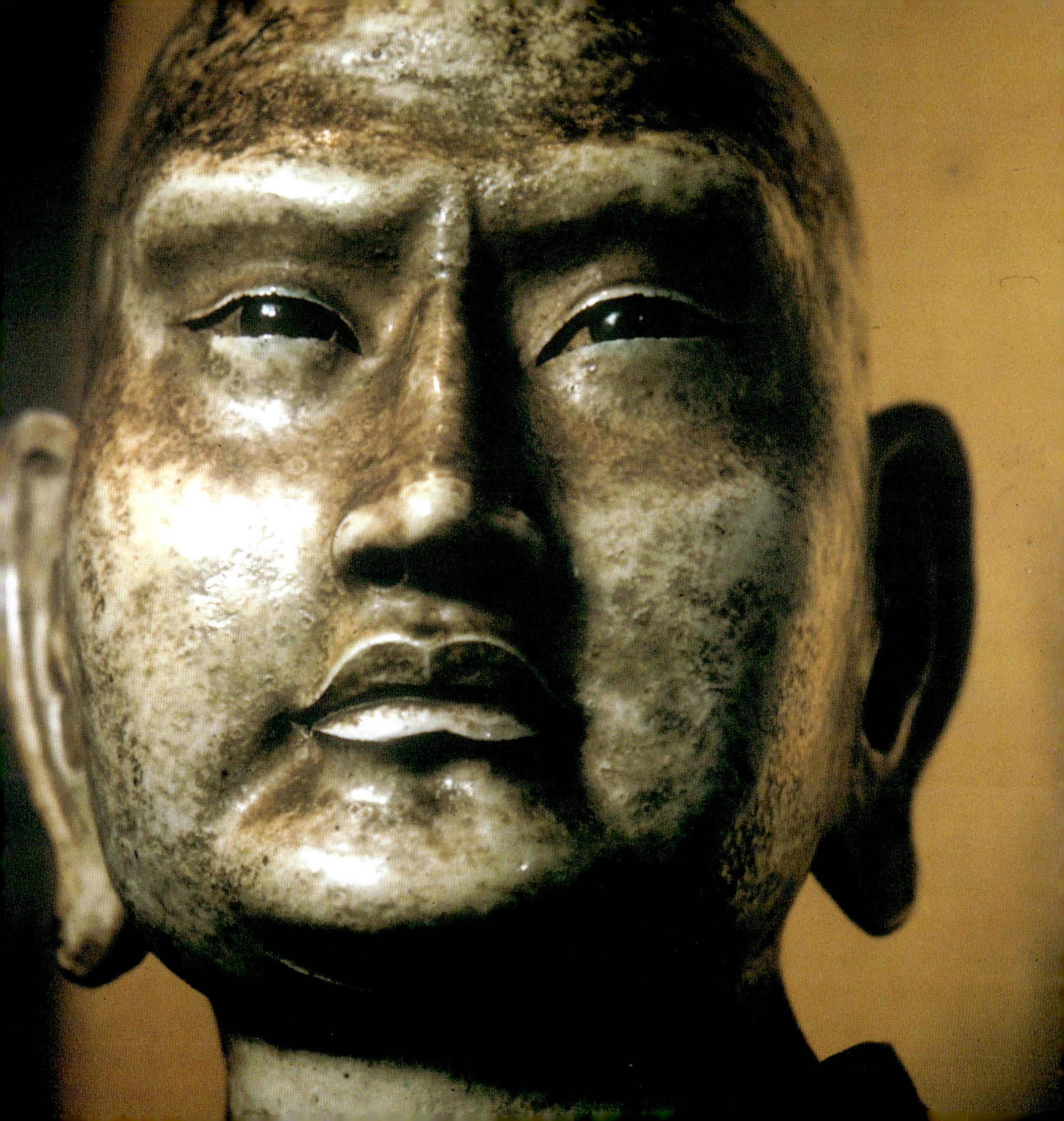

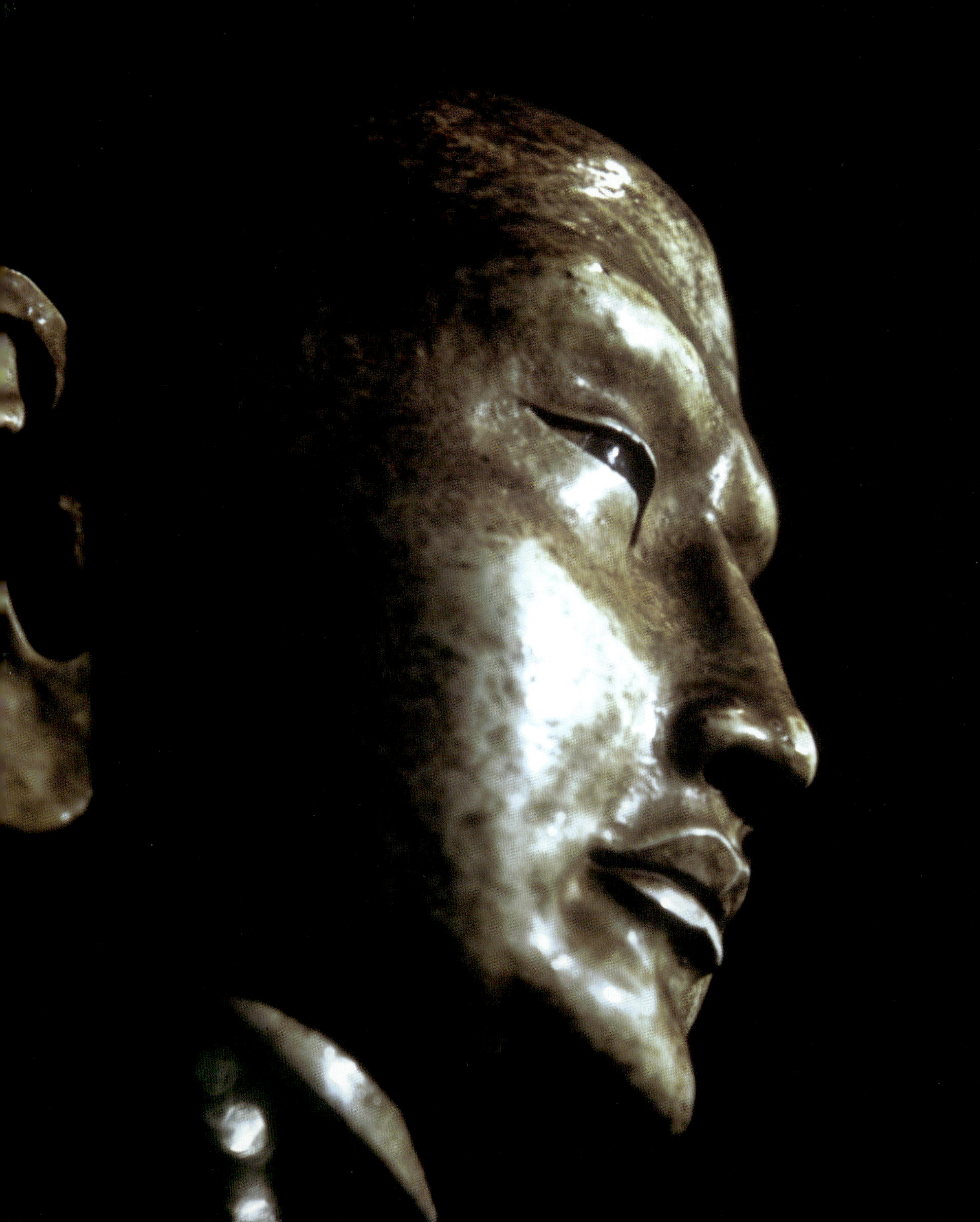

By the time these Lohans were made, ceramics had been one of China's greatest industries for centuries. Chinese ceramic work was in international demand from the T'ang Dynasty onwards. For such large, comissioned religious statues, the low-temperature kilns they were fired in could have been available almost anywhere in China, since such kilns were relatively easy to construct.

There are many T'ang chronicle listings of dedications and praises of 16 and 18 statue Lohan sets. Some of the statues were ceramic. Among those were some great works of art. What other masterpieces were produced by the artist of the I-Chou Lohan statues? He probably made more than one lohan set in his lifetime and he probably made statues of the Buddha, images of complete realization. Buddhist art forms had limited development in India. Buddhism was to be devastated by invasions in its homeland, but the Buddha's realization teachings were transmitted successfully into other nations. In three northern nations—China,

LOHAN ONE

Portrait of Priest Mangan. Hakone Shrine, Kanagawa Prefecture. The priest practiced on several sacred mountains of the Kanto districts. Died in 816 AD. The statue is a masterpiece of the period, carved out of wood.

Tibet, and Japan—there developed traditions of life-like art representing the Buddha's disciples and teachers of the lineages, those who assumed the meditation posture and transmissions.

Suzuki Roshi on the posture of sitting practice:
"The state of mind that exists when you sit in the right posture is, itself, enlightenment...You should not be tilted sideways, backwards, or forwards. You should be sitting up as if you were supporting the sky with your head. This is not just form or breathing. It expresses the key point of Buddhism. It is a perfect expression of your Buddhanature. If you want true understanding of Buddhism, you should practice this way. These forms are not a means of obtaining the right state of mind. To take this posture itself is the purpose of practice. When you have this posture, you have the right state of mind, so there is no need to attain some special state." [10]

[10] Suzuki, Roshi. Zen Mind, Beginner's Mind, Weatherhill, New York and Tokyo, 1970, p.26.

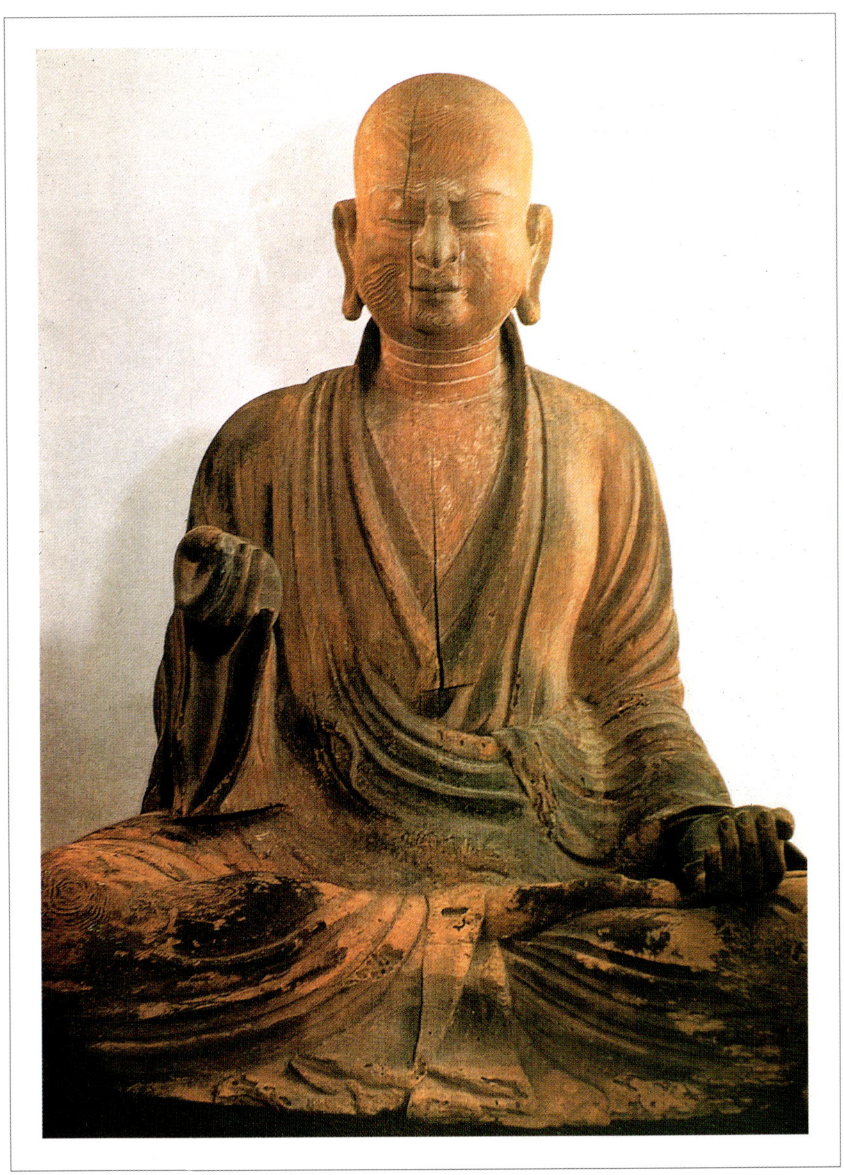

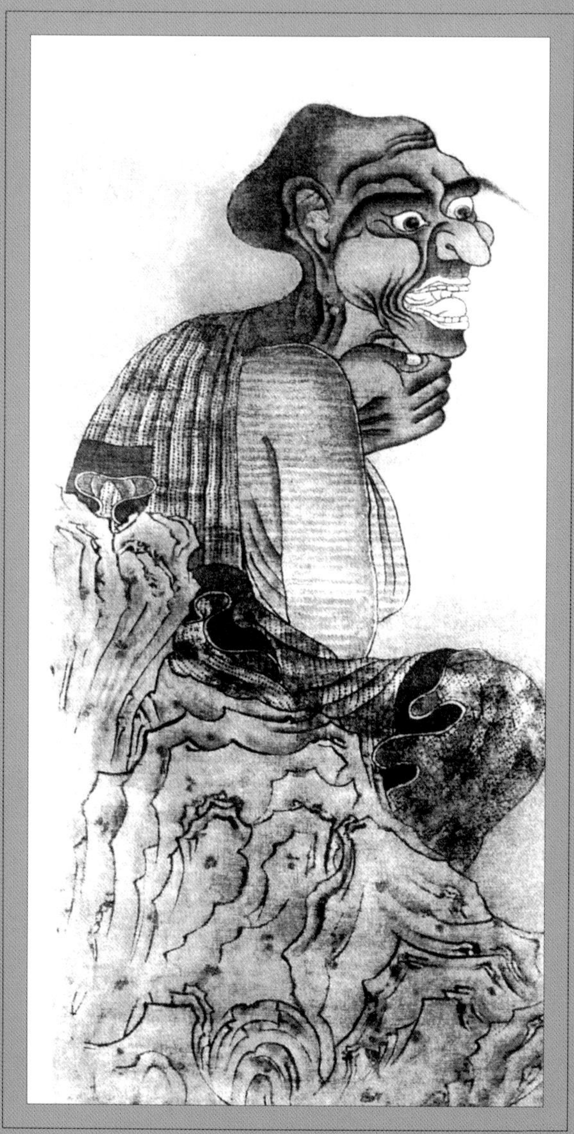

ARHATS IN SCRIPTURE AND LITERATURE

LOHAN, KUAN-HSIU, 10th century ink and paint on silk. "Chan master" Kuan-Hsiu set of 16 images was legendary. His Lohans are caricatures rendered with great facilty and feeling. They were an important influence on Chinese painting.

Arhat (arhant), Skt. (Pali, arahat; Chin., lohan; Jap., rakan); "worthy one" who has attained the highest level on the supramundane path by extinguishing habit patterns obstructive to evolutionary development. The arhat will not have to be born in samsara again. In the early Buddhist scriptures, Buddha is said to have called himself Arhat. An Arhat had the Six Supernormal Talents developed by Shakyamuni the night before he became completely awakened: 1) divine eye; 2) divine hearing; 3) knowledge of the hearts and thoughts of others; 4) knowledge of former existences of oneself and others; 5) dominion over one's body at will, the power of assuming any shape; and 6) exhaustion of leaking* (drying up the outflows). The outflows are dried up through meditation. The energy of attention is shifted from mind to open awareness. Instead of flowing out through the actions of body, speech and mind, the meditator's attention is absorbed in open awareness.

---

*"leaking": wasting ones psychic energies by mechanically feeding them to the impulses of mind, so that one doesn't have the energy for greater function.

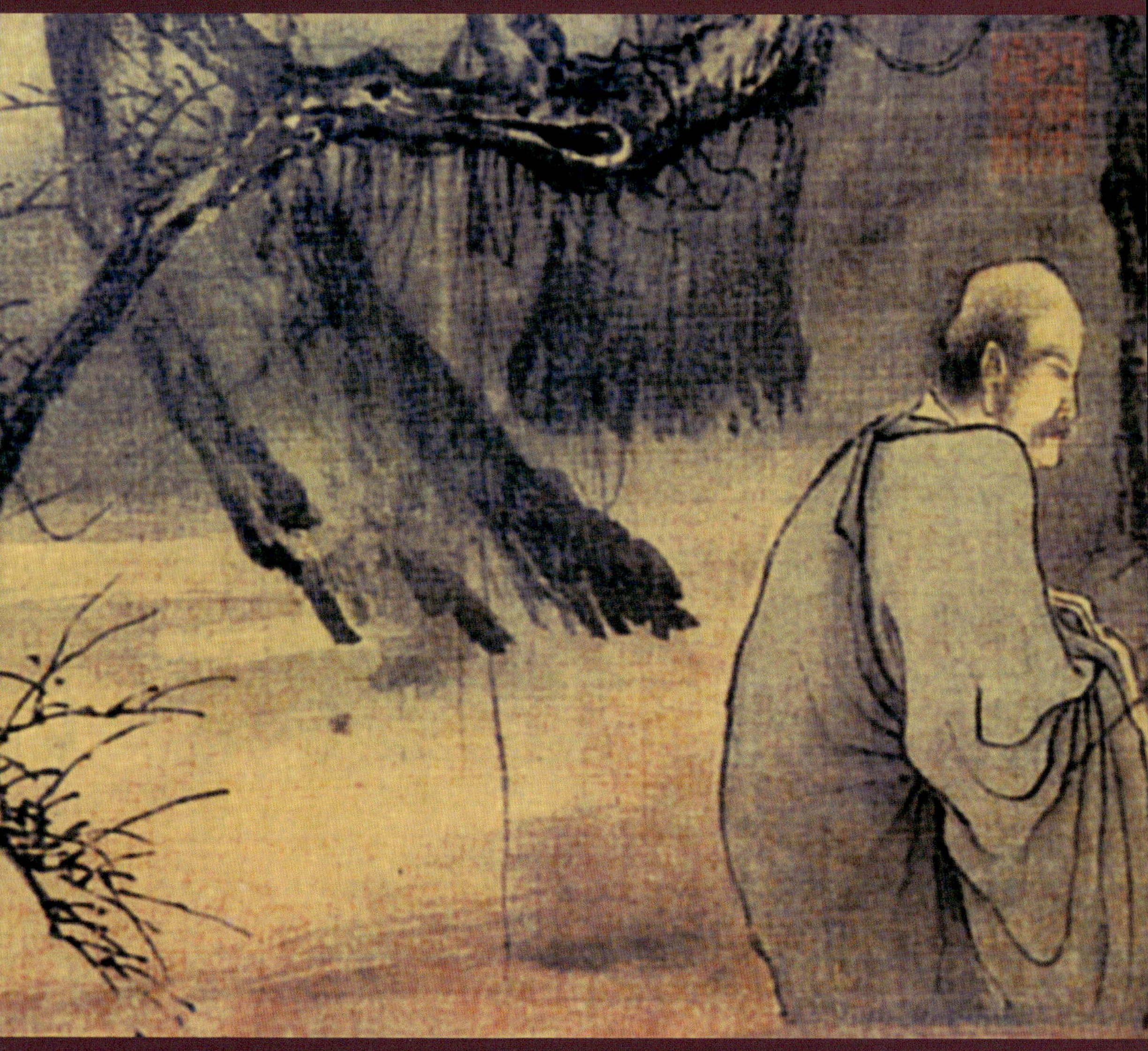

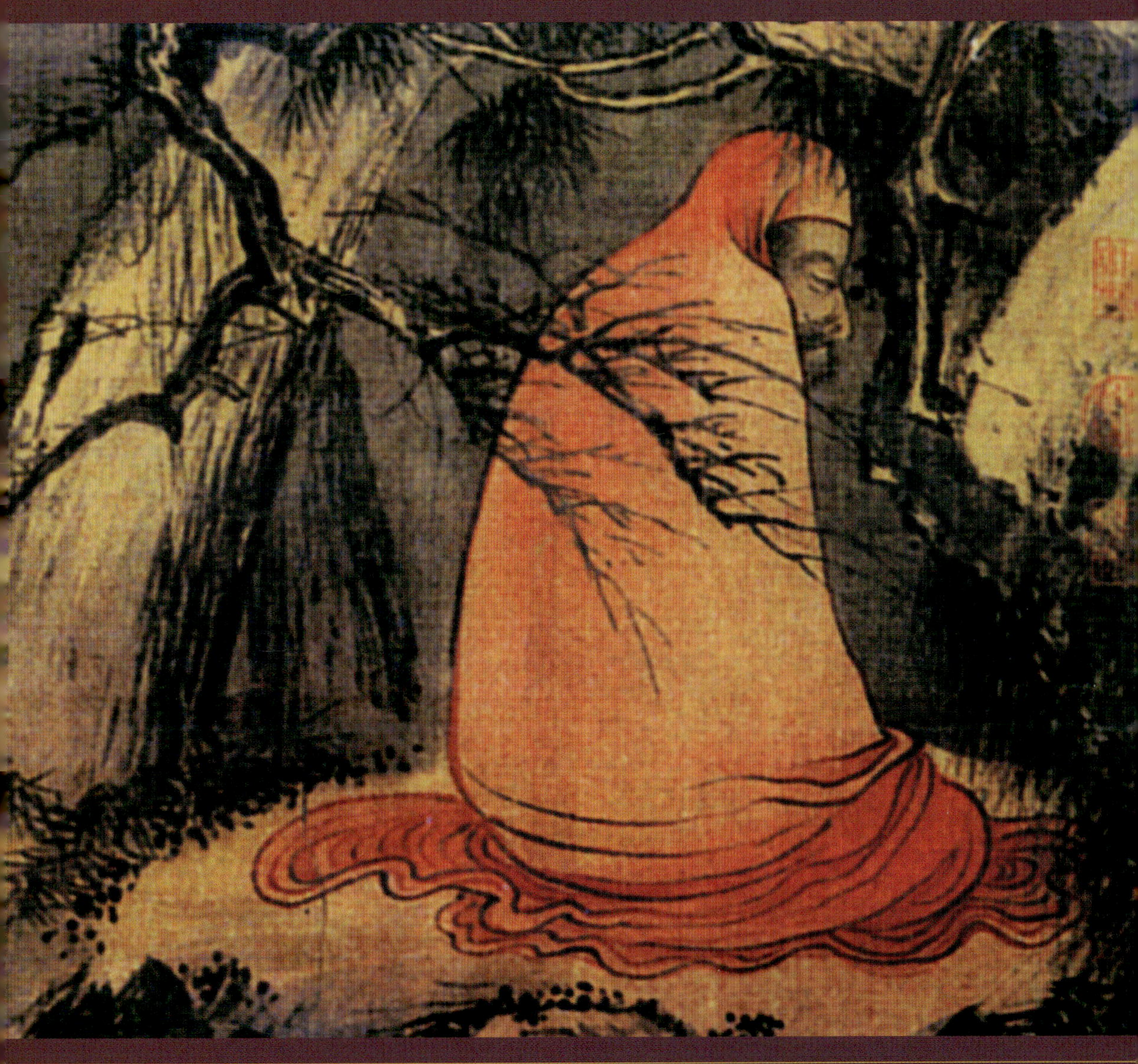

G KAI: EIGHT EMINENT MONKS: Bodhidharma Facing A Wall. Ink and color on silk, Shanghai Museum C 1000 AD.

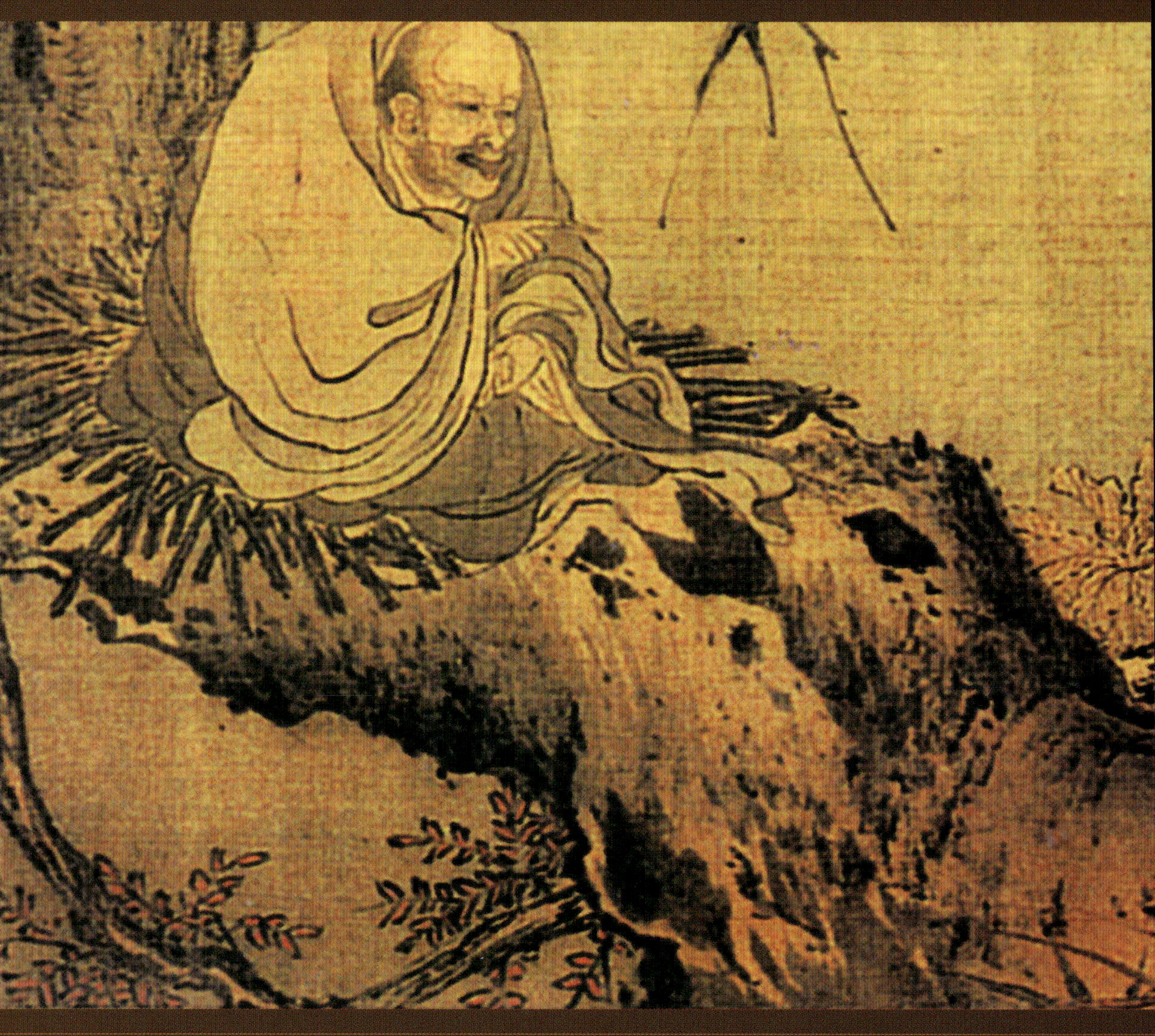

Liang Kai: Eight Eminent Monks: Bai Suji calling on Monk Niaoke
Ink and color on silk, Shanghai Museum C 1000 AD

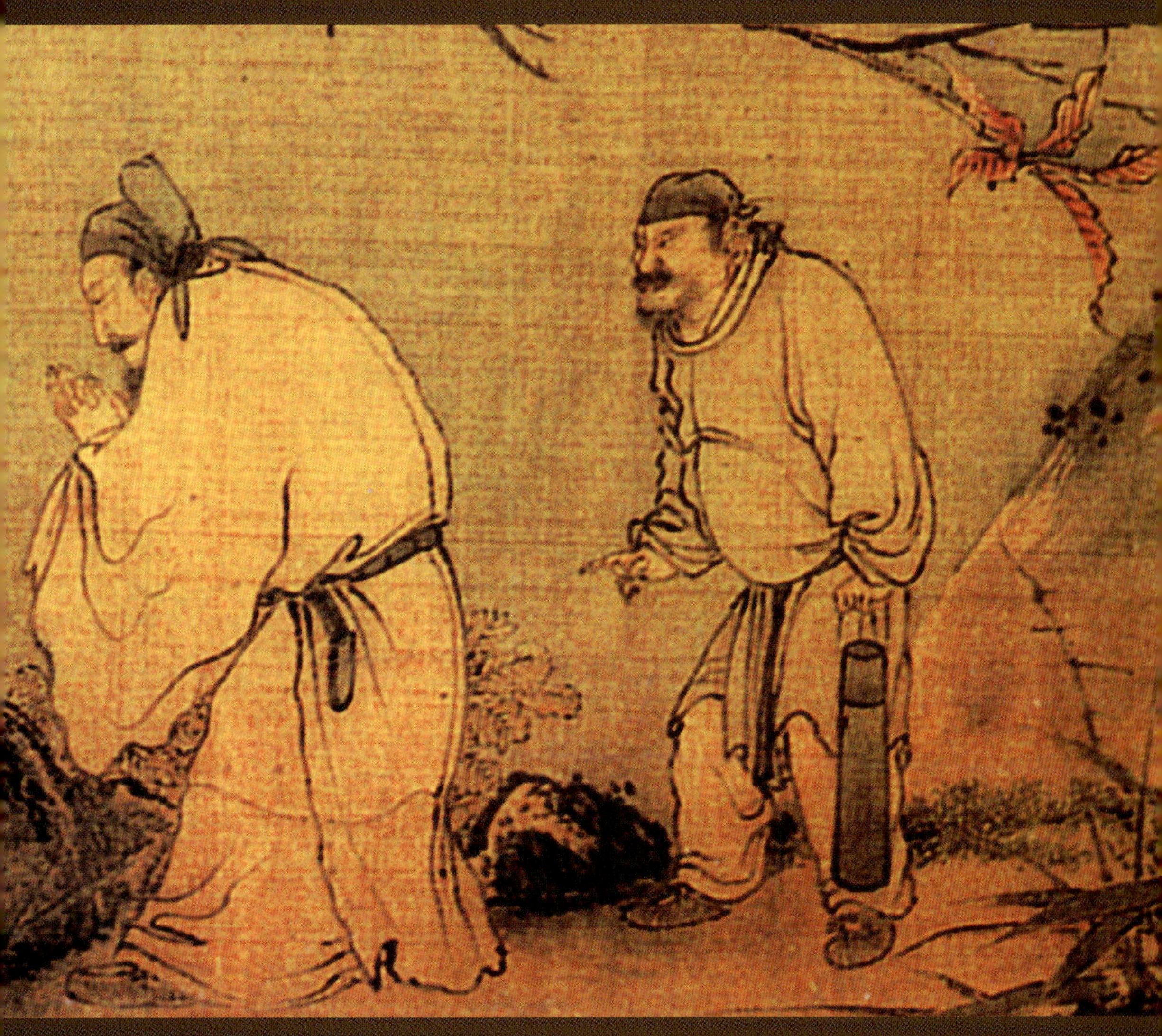

TUNG-HUANG cave 196, 8th century. Kasyapa standing between the buddha and a bodhisattva.

When the tendency to feed energy to the movements of mind has been reduced, the meditator gains some stability in awareness. Energy is then available for higher functions. Arhats are famous for their demonstrations of power.

With the development of Mahayana Buddhism, in the 1st and 2nd C AD, the arhat ideal was considered to be selfish and somewhat limited compared to the bodhisattva ideal. The Arhat was said to have 37 supermundane qualities that a bodhisattva has, but the bodhisattva was seen to have greater realization potential, based on compassionate connection to all life. It's in the human potential to realize unlimited skills in serving life in all realms. The I-Chou Lohans represent Buddhist discipline with vows of refuge, compassion and service in the bodhisattva ideal. The statues are permeated with expressions of compassion and the openness to a greater life.

From Ming times onward, in the slow decline of spiritual authority in China, the lohan statues made for new monasteries became increasingly reflective of folk traditions. Various legendary figures were given the long buddha ears of the lohans. As Buddhism's influence diminished in China, lohan statue groups became predominantly '500 Lohan' groups.* There are '500 Lohan' halls in surviving Chinese monasteries. Massive galleries are full of life-size figures with various characteristic attributes and expressions. In the expanded iconog-

*Substantially less than 500 statues

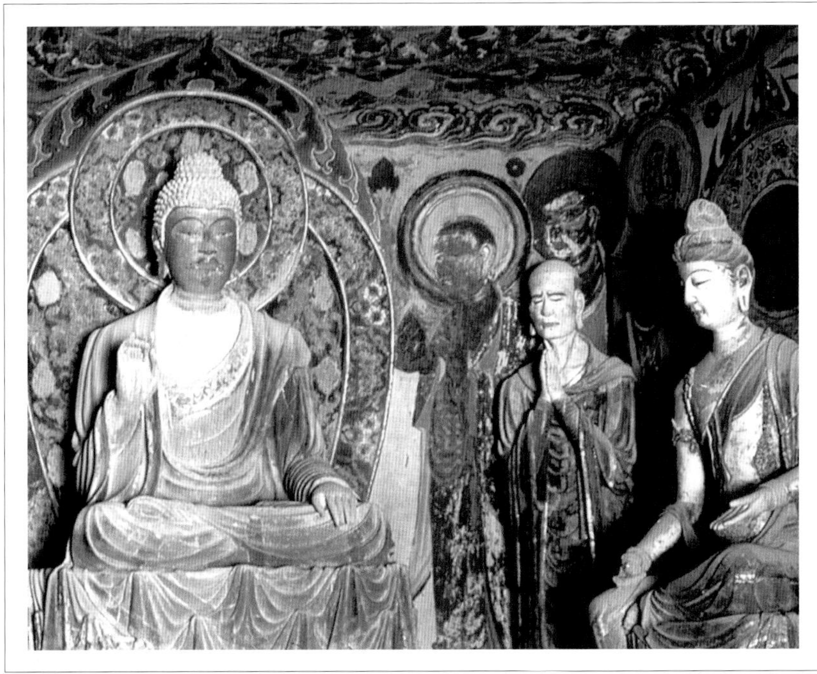

raphy of the later lohan sets, there are non-Buddhist figures from Chinese folklore. There is even Marco Polo.

Apparently the 500 Lohan concept is derived from a Pali canon scripture concerning the first great council after the Parinirvana. Kasyapa selected 500 Arhats to carry the Teaching. In China, eventually 500 lohans became "guardians of the sanctuaries." Thus at the time of the creation of the I-Chou Lohans there was the early tradition of the two lohans of the buddha pentad; there was a well established tradition of the 16 or 18 lohans; and there was a "500 Lohan" tradition.

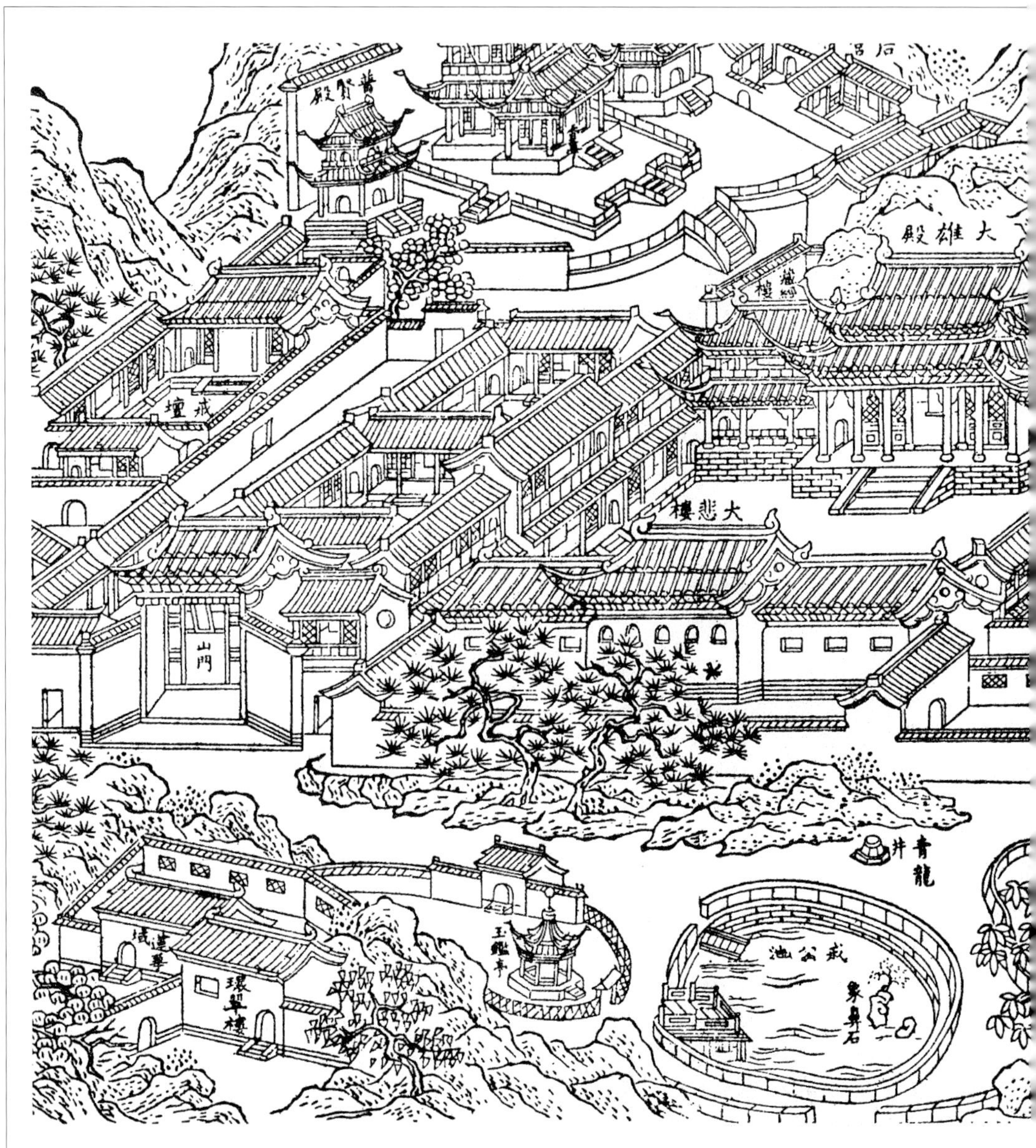
普賢殿
大雄殿
藏經樓
戒壇
大悲樓
山門
青龍井
戒公池
象鼻石
玉鑑亭
蓮華域
環翠樓

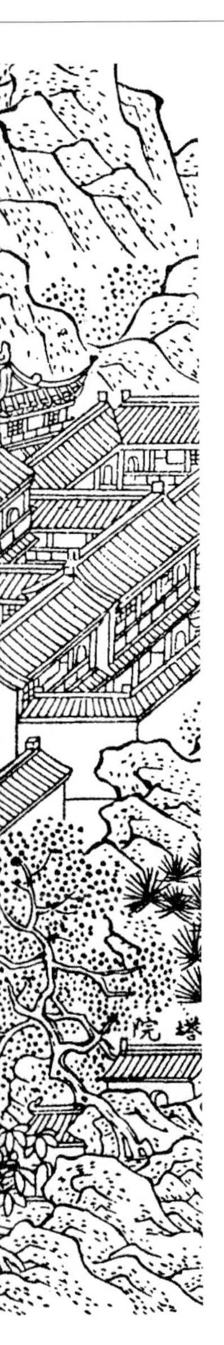

Mahayana Training Halls: Huichu-Ssu Monastery (opposite)

In the monasteries of Ch'an Buddhism, universal buddhahood was being taught and fully practiced. In the evolution of the Ch'an monasteries, sculptured imagery was used throughout the buildings.

Huichu-Ssu Monastery from above (below)

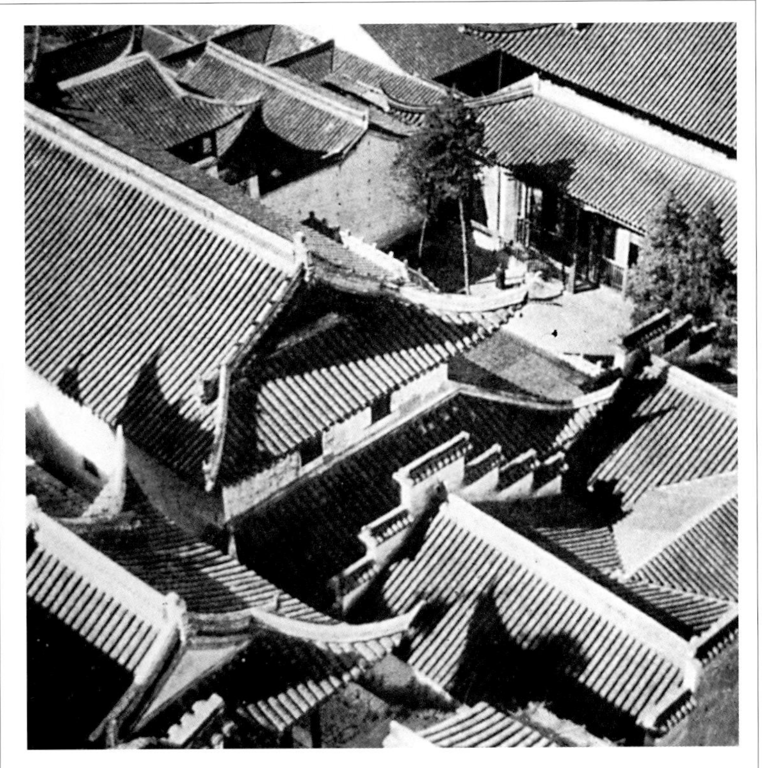

Lohan, Ling-Yan- Si Monastery.
China, Ming Dynasty, painted wood. One of 22 life size Lohans, made for a hall of their own. They show that the tradition was alive and well, still profound, beyond the Sung and into the Ming Dynasty.

Ling-Yan- Si Lohans
opposite page

Somewhere in the middle of the lohan-disciple tradition are the I-Chou Lohans. Looking at them, we can't tell which disciples the artist had in mind. In general they show us images of a life devoted to meditation, free of name, nation and inner state.

In the beginning of the lohan tradition, in Gandhara, (see p. 66) both the buddha image and the disciple image had the same large ears, with elongated earlobes, a traditional way of representing one of the physical characteristics of a buddha. In Northern Buddhism in general, all representations of disciples or teachers

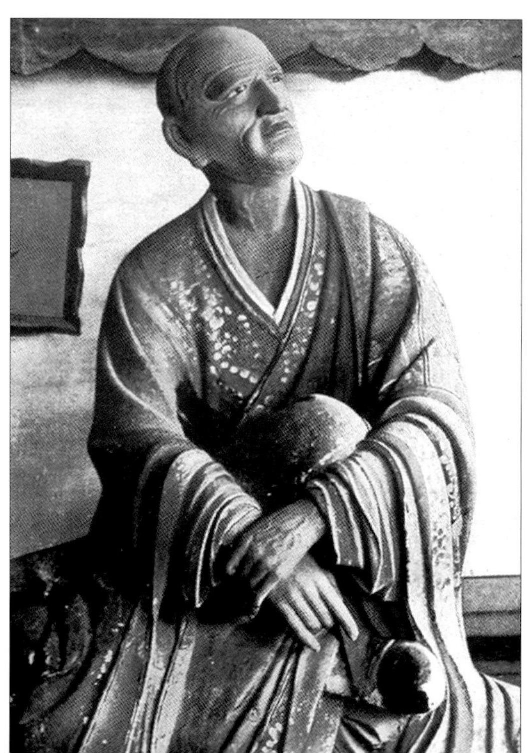

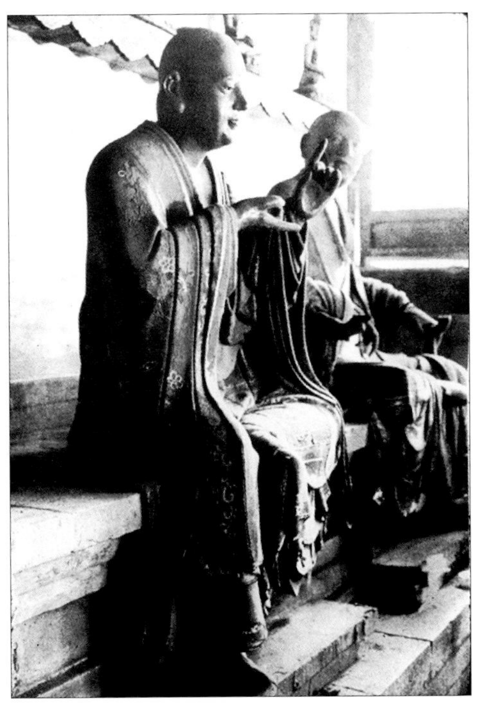

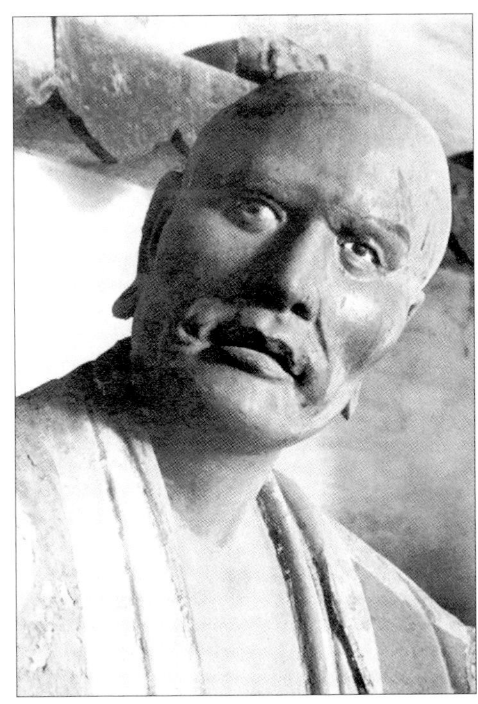

those that had heard the Buddha's doctrine—had large 'buddha ears'. The lohan images represent humans evolving. The human body is a buddha form.

Sixteen Arhats are mentioned in the *Treatise on Entering Mahayana Buddhism*, translated by Tao Tai of the Northern Liang Dynasty (397 to 439 AD). Another mention of the Sixteen Arhats is in the *Suddharma-Pundarika-Sutra* translated by Chan Jan in the Eighth Century. The Sixteen Arhats are entrusted to carry and

Interior, Ling-Yan-Si Monastery

Lohan statues were in the shrines of Chinese Buddhist monasteries, and were often a support for meditation, along with iconic Buddhas

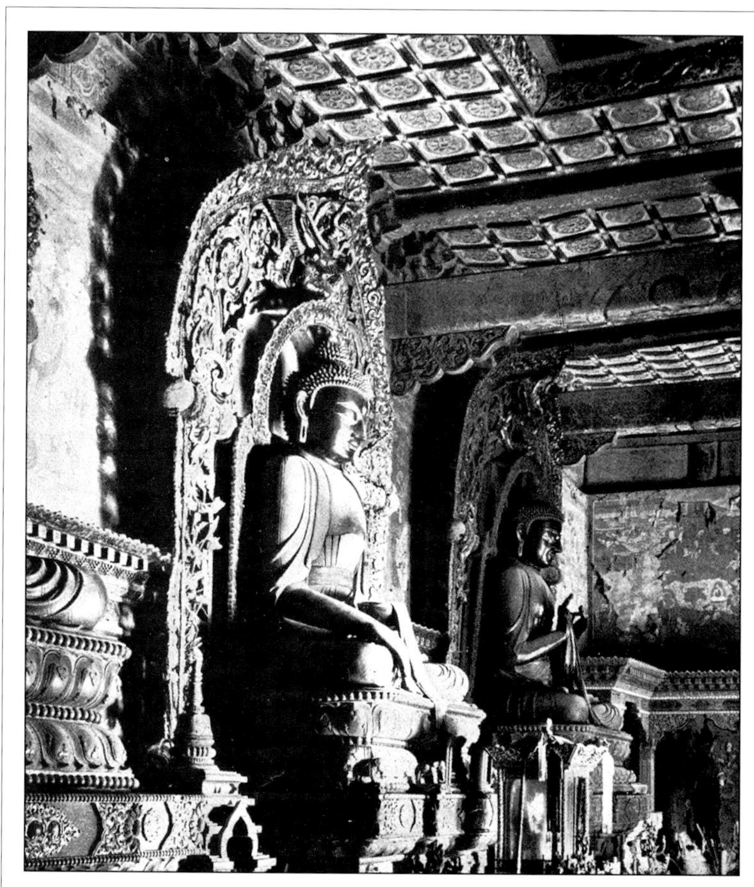

500 Lohan T'ang interior,

(opposite page)
Kuangtung, Canton, China. Some Chinese Buddhist monasteries surviving into the 20th century had '500 Lohan' halls. The sheer mass of the statues is impressive, each with its individual gesture or pose representing a legendary figure. Most of these later lohan were inclusions from Chinese culture.

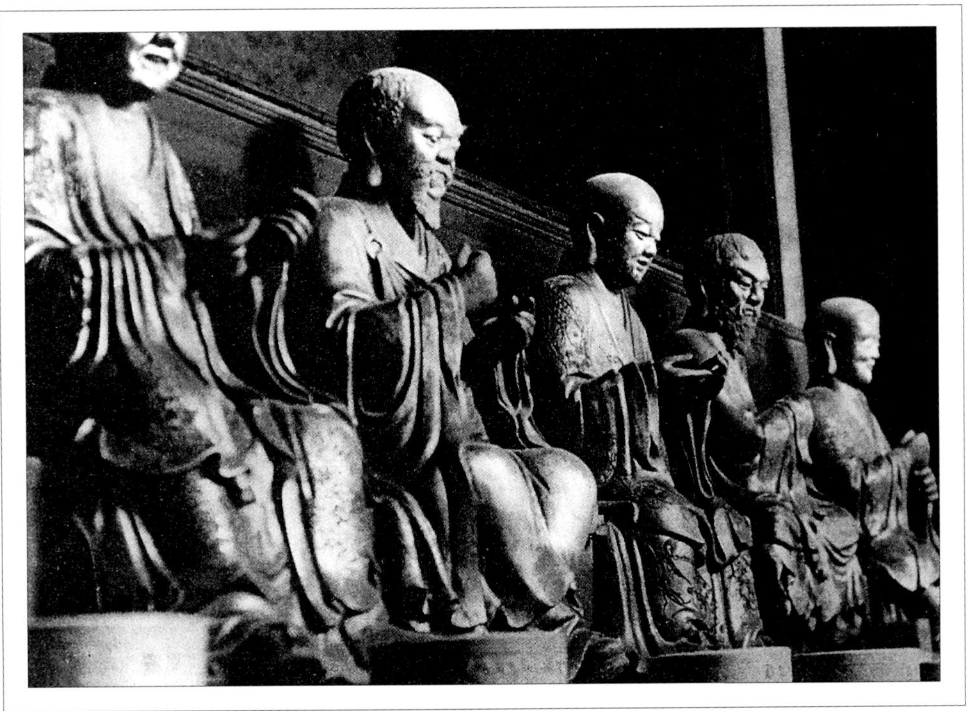

sustain the Dharma throughout the four quarters of the world.

Though the legend of the Sixteen Arhats had been known in China, it was after the translation of the *Record of the Abiding of the Law* by Hsuan Tsang (645 AD) that they became widely popular among Chinese Buddhists. This book belongs to the miscellaneous

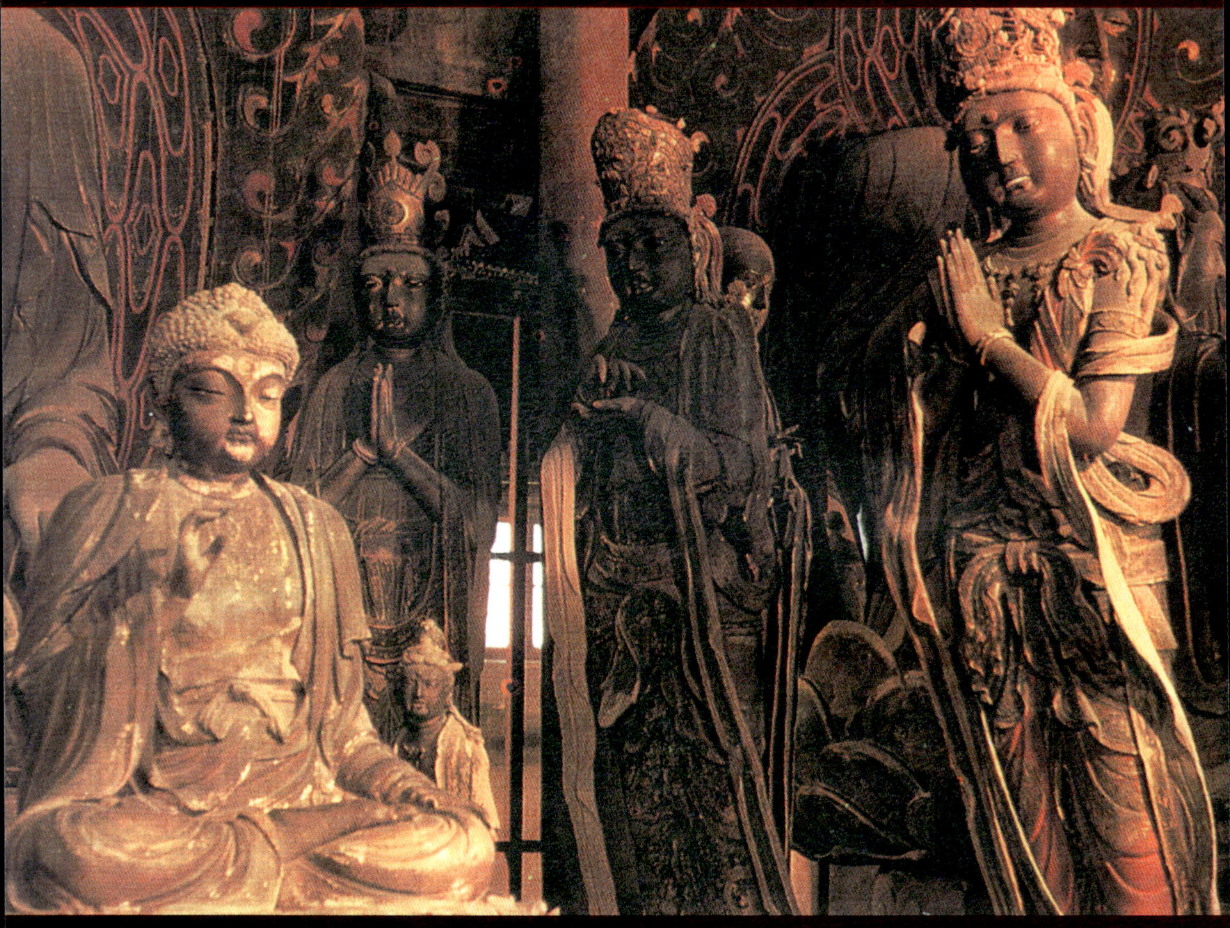

In the Presence of the Buddha. Interior Ta-T'ung, Shansi, China. Liao Dynasty, 1038 AD.

works of the Canon. Its full title is *Record on the Abiding of the Law in This World Explained by the Great Arhat Nandimitra* .

The Record may be the most extensive scriptural source of arhat information. "The Buddha, when about to enter Parinirvana, entrusted the Supreme Law to the Sixteen Great Arhats and their relatives (followers), ordering them to protect and maintain it and to prevent it from being extinguished....These Sixteen Great Arhats are all provided with the three *Vidyas*, the six *Abhijnas* (kinds of transcendental knowledge), the eight *Vimokshas*, etc., immeasurable gifts and virtues. They have separated themselves from the infection of the three worlds (of desire, form and formlessness), recite and maintain the *Tripitaka* and are all versed in the outer canons (rules not belonging to the doctrine). They have received the Buddha's command (to stay on this side of *Nirvana**and protect the Law). By means of the power of transcendental knowledge they lengthen their own lives. As long as the Buddha's *Suddharma* shall remain (in the world)... [the Arhats will] appear in all kinds of

---

* i.e. either to keep reincarnating as a teacher or to live long lives. Ancient arhats are believed still at large in the world.

† DeVisser, Marius Willem, *The Arhats in China and Japan*, Berlin, Orsterhelk & Co., p. 78.

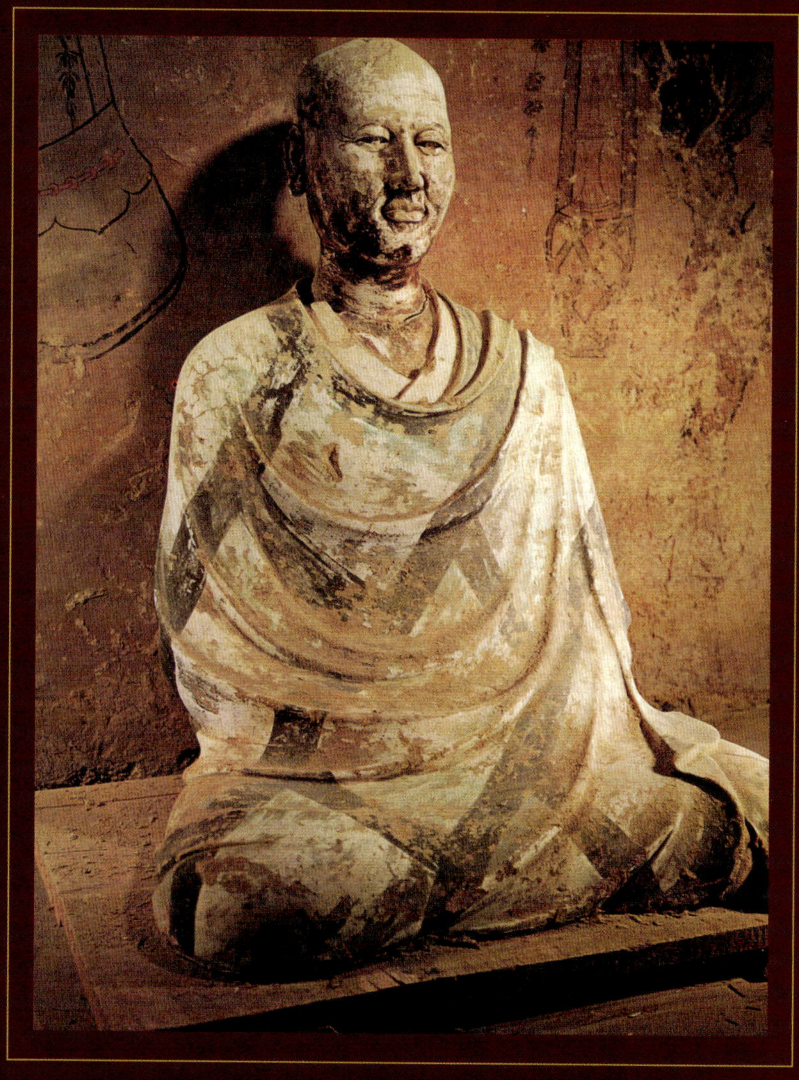

Statue of Hong Bian, Tun-Huang, cave 17 (the documents cave)
Early 8th century

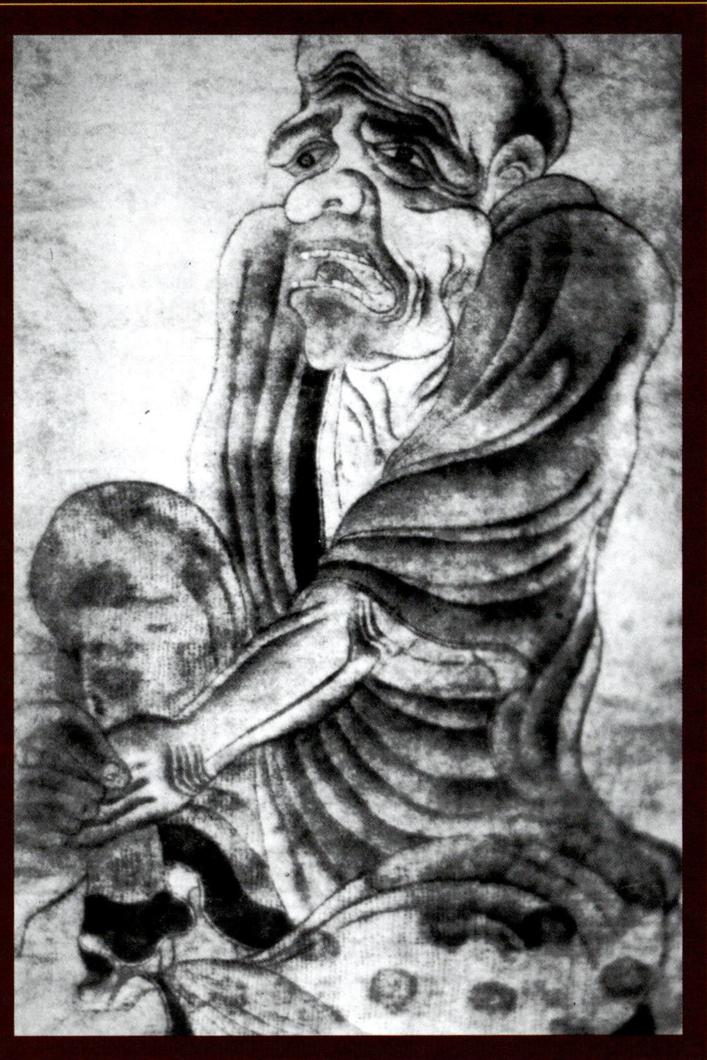

KUAN-HSIU LOHAN, 10th Century ink and color on silk

Kuan-Hsiu's art contrasts well with the I-Chou Lohans. Between the statues and his paintings we get a vivid sense of the lohan tradition in its prime.

shapes, hiding their holy attitude and being like the common crowd."[†] More specific information about the Sixteen Arhats is only given in terms of their names and abodes, the regions in which their work for the Dharma was performed.

Although the descriptions in *The Record* are limited, in Mahayana and Theravadan books there are references to stories about some of the arhats. From those stories and studies of Chinese lohan imagery, T. Waters wrote of iconographic features in his book, *The Eighteen Lohan of Chinese Buddhist Temples*, for example: (1) Pindola; a successful disputant and defender of orthodox ways.... Weakness for exhibiting his magical powers before all kinds of people.... Miracles wrought for good and bad purposes.... Pindola is still alive; appears to pious workers for Buddhism. Flying old man with long eyebrows. Holding scripture or alms bowl reverentially in both hands or an open scripture on one knee and a mendicant's staff at his side....(4) Subhinda; venerable old sage with a scroll in his right hand or sitting in meditation. Also with alms bowl and incense vase, holding a sacred book in the left hand. Snapping his fingers, indicative of the rapidity with which he attained spiritual insight.[*]

---

[*] Waters, Thomas. *The 18 Lohan of Chinese Buddhist Temples*. Shanghai (Kelly & Wals), 1925.

[†] Wen Fong. *The Lohans and a Bridge to Heaven,* Washington, DC, 1958, p. 37.

In *The Record* two of the four original Great Arhats, Kasyapa and Kundopadhaniya are omitted. Wen Fong has a discussion of the Theravada-Mahayana controversy implicit in the list in *The Record* and its omissions.† The concept of arhatship proves to be somewhat central in the "Great Schism" in the development of Buddhism. It is in focus for the Mahayana system in formulating the bodhisattva ideal. The arhat is considered selfish and seen to be intent upon his or her own personal salvation. The bodhisattva, the new ideal, postpones his or her own salvation to work for all sentient beings. Even though the I-Chou Lohans are arhats, they express the bodhisattva ideal.

Hobson proposed that the British Museum lohan was "Sohinda Sonja" (Subhinda), but identification of the I-Chou Lohans with arhats mentioned in the scriptures is difficult. One might project that the youngest looking of the remaining I-Chou Lohans (LOHAN THREE) is Ananda and that LOHAN TWO is Kasyapa, both of them having facial characteristics similar to the Ananda and Kasyapa figures found frequently in the Chinese cave-shrines and in Gandhara. However, the I-Chou Lohan faces don't need names. They were made to convey the external and internal presence of the Buddha.

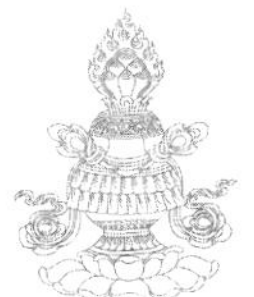

Gandhara is the ancient name of a region which extended from Bamiyan in the west and from the Swat valley in Afghanistan through the Peshawar and Rawalpindi districts of northwestern Pakistan. Gandhara was a crossroads of commerce, a meeting ground of various cultural worlds, India, Central Asia, the Middle East and the West. The first known references to Gandhara go back to the Rig Veda, about 1,200 C. BC. The Swat

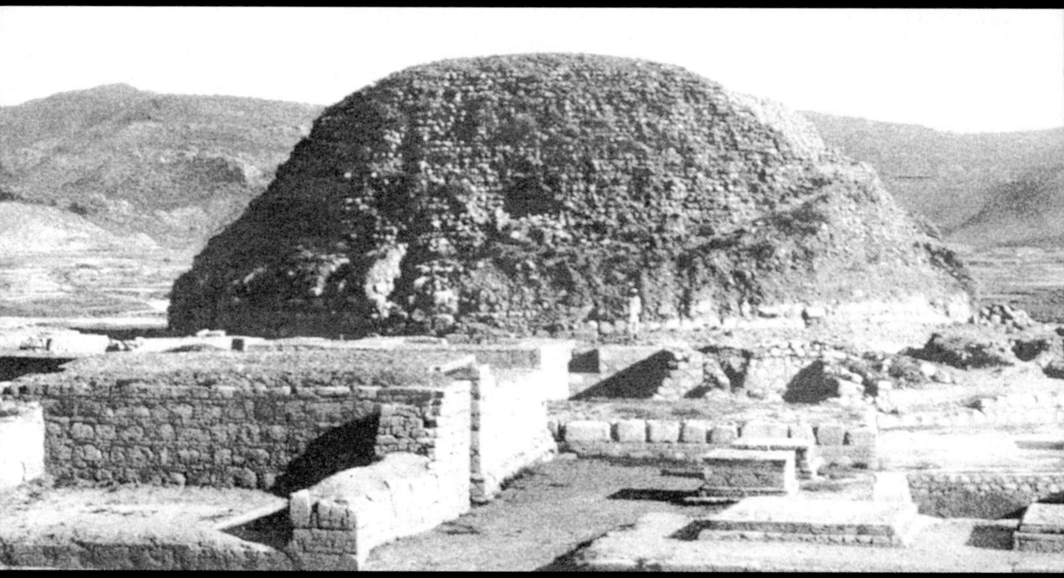

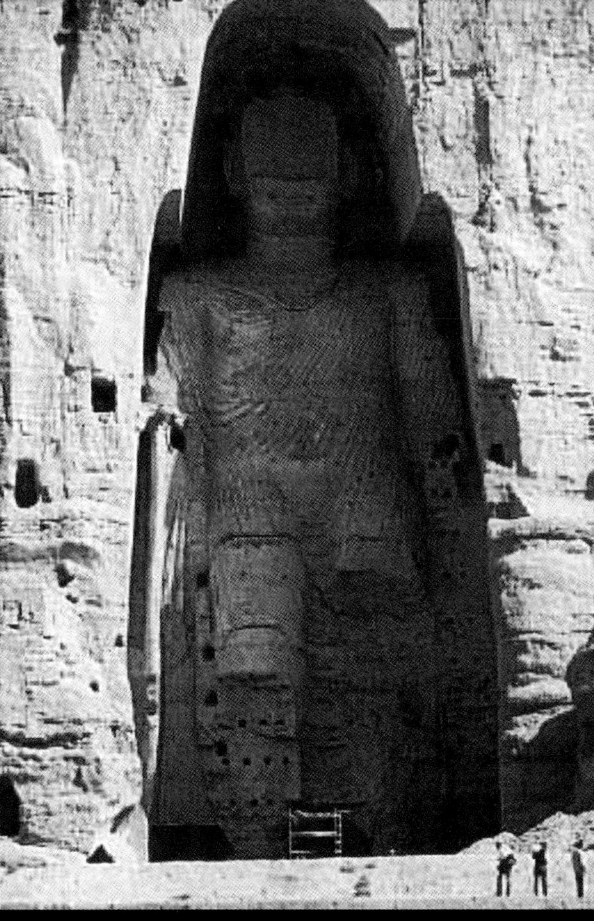

Remains of the Great Stupa at Taxila, Gandhara, with excavated temple sites. 1st-2th C AD. (opposite page)

Bamiyan, Gandhara. 1st-2nd C AD. Colossal standing Buddha, 120 ft high. Just before it was destroyed by the Taliban, in 2001.

Valley contained evolutionary schools, perhaps from very ancient traditions. The region became famous as a center of Buddhism in association with the Indian king Ashoka, who converted to Buddhism in the 3rd C. BC. It was the meeting ground of Eastern and Western traditions. Gandhara remained Buddhist, disseminating the Dharma into present day Afghanistan and Central Asia until the 5th C AD. It is associated with preeminent teachers and seats of Mahayana Buddhism from the 1st

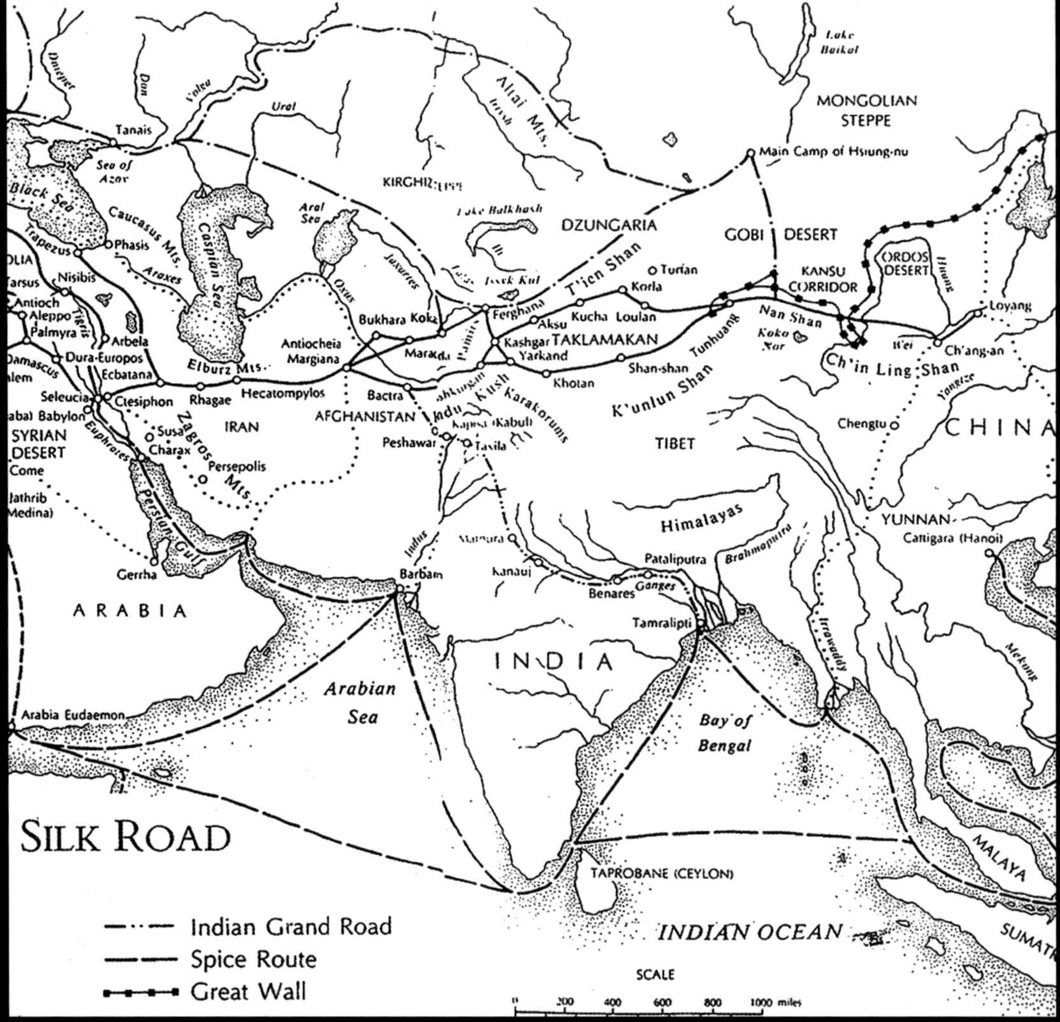
SILK ROAD
Indian Grand Road
Spice Route
Great Wall
SCALE
0 200 400 600 800 1000 miles
MONGOLIAN STEPPE
Lake Baikal
Main Camp of Hsiung-nu
Altai Mts.
Dnieper
Don
Volga
Ural
Tanais
Sea of Azov
Black Sea
Caucasus Mts.
Caspian Sea
Aral Sea
Lake Balkhash
DZUNGARIA
GOBI DESERT
T'ien Shan
Turfan
KANSU CORRIDOR
ORDOS DESERT
Korla
Kucha
Loulan
Aksu
Ferghana
Kashgar
TAKLAMAKAN
Yarkand
Khotan
Shan-shan
Tunhuang
Nan Shan
Koko Nor
Loyang
Ch'ang-an
Wei
Ch'in Ling Shan
K'unlun Shan
Yangtze
Chengtu
CHINA
TIBET
Karakorums
Trapezus
Phasis
Araxes
Nisibis
Tarsus
Antioch
Aleppo
Palmyra
Tigris
Arbela
Damascus
Dura-Europos
Ecbatana
Elburz Mts.
Seleucia
Ctesiphon
Babylon
Euphrates
Rhagae
Hecatompylos
Antiocheia Margiana
Bukhara
Oxus
Jaxartes
Bactra
AFGHANISTAN
IRAN
Susa
Zagros Mts.
Charax
Persepolis
SYRIAN DESERT
Come
Jathrib (Medina)
Persian Gulf
Gerrha
ARABIA
Peshawar
Indus
Barbaricum
Kanauj
Himalayas
Pataliputra
Brahmaputra
Benares
Ganges
Tamralipti
INDIA
Irrawaddy
Mekong
YUNNAN
Cattigara (Hanoi)
Arabian Sea
Bay of Bengal
Arabia Eudaemon
TAPROBANE (CEYLON)
INDIAN OCEAN
MALAYA

to the 4th C AD. Padmasambhava, "The Second Buddha", the one who brought Vajrayana Buddhadharma to Tibet in the 8th C AD was born in Oddiyana, "The Northwest Region", associated with the Swat Valley.

From the time that the buddha image was first developed in Gandhara and Mathura, images of the Buddha's disciples were present in the 12 main events of the Buddha's life. There was always the buddha in the

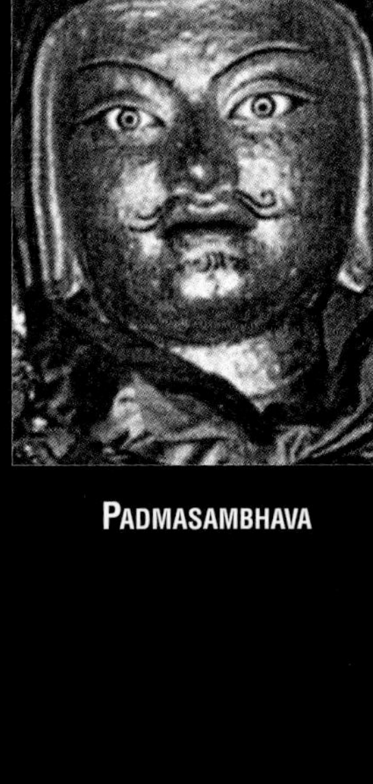

Padmasambhava

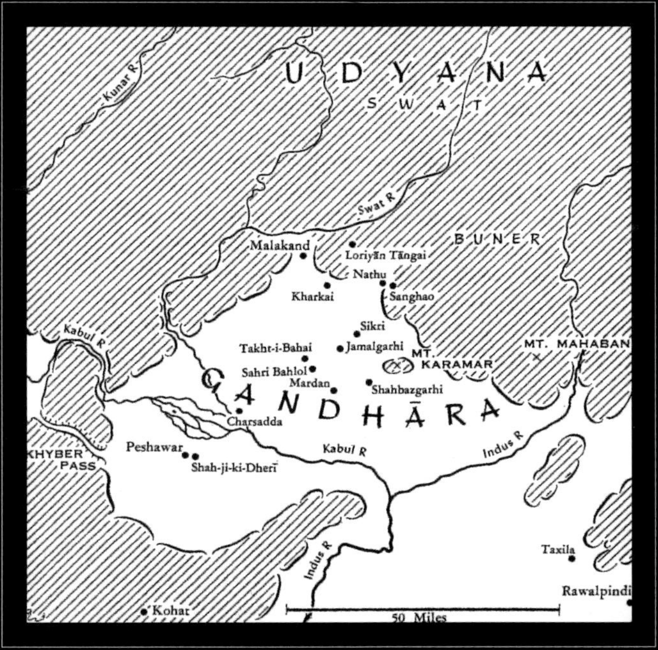

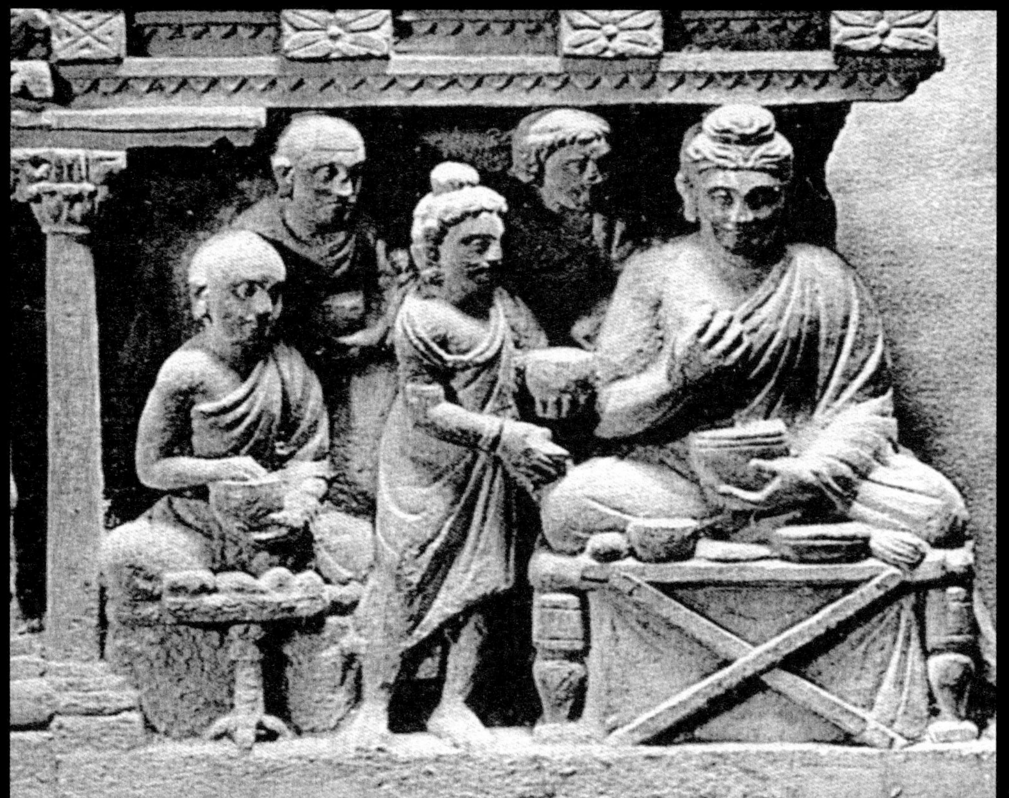

THE FIRST SERMON, GANDHARA, 1st C AD. Carved stonework,

center, usually in meditation posture. Around him the robed monk disciples were depicted, sometimes shown in meditation posture. The imagery of the Buddha and his disciples developed in the stone relief sculpture around stupas in the first and second C AD. The story was Indian* but the art looked western, particularly Greek. The Gandharan stupas and stone craft centers were largely in the Peshawar Valley and neighboring tracts west of the Indus river where the schist and other fine-grained stone were quarried. In that period of work on the stupa imagery, sensitive character differentiation appeared in the Life-of-the-Buddha art. There is careful facial delineation in some of the disciples. That is the beginning of the lohan-disciple tradition.

The imagery from the Life-of-the-Buddha was central to the second phase of Gandharan art, beginning in the 4th C AD. This was the period of the development of Buddhist statuary shrines. Statues of disciples were beside the shrine buddha, all showing the influence of western figurative art, representing divine being in human form.

---

*Jakata Tales. Ancient Indian folk tales, adapted by Buddhism to read as stories of the earlier incarnations of the Buddha.

Buddha in Meditation Posture, Gandhara,
1st-2nd C AD.
Stone relief, H. 50"

On the Silk Route in Bamiyan, Gandhara, the colossal image of the Buddha and the excavated temples were striking to pilgrims and merchants going to and coming from China. In the multitude of statues throughout the rock-cut halls and chapels at Bamiyan, there were many statues representing meditation.

The Buddhist figures at Bamiyan are said to have been direct models for the clay-surfaced colossal buddhas of the first Chinese excavated mountains. Gandhara was alive with Buddhist imagery; knowledge of it was taken into China and fully developed.

Buddhist scriptures and images were brought into China both by the few Chinese who left and then were able to eventually return to China with them, and by Buddhist monks like Kuamarajiva, who came from Buddhist central Asia to China in 401 AD with many books and some objects. From the second half of the Fourth Century, the new Buddhist art flourished in Gandhara, until the destruction of the Buddhist monasteries and monuments at the hands of the White Huns, about 465 AD. The impact and transmission of Buddhist art had gone into China.

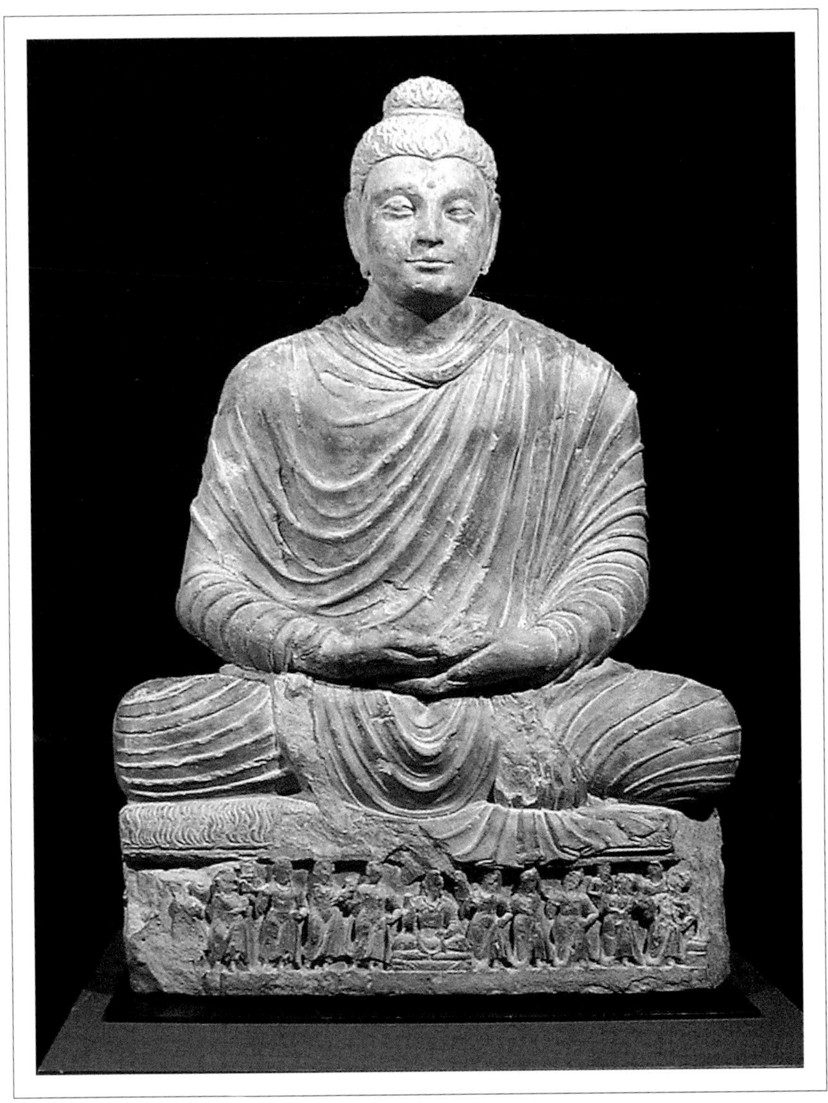

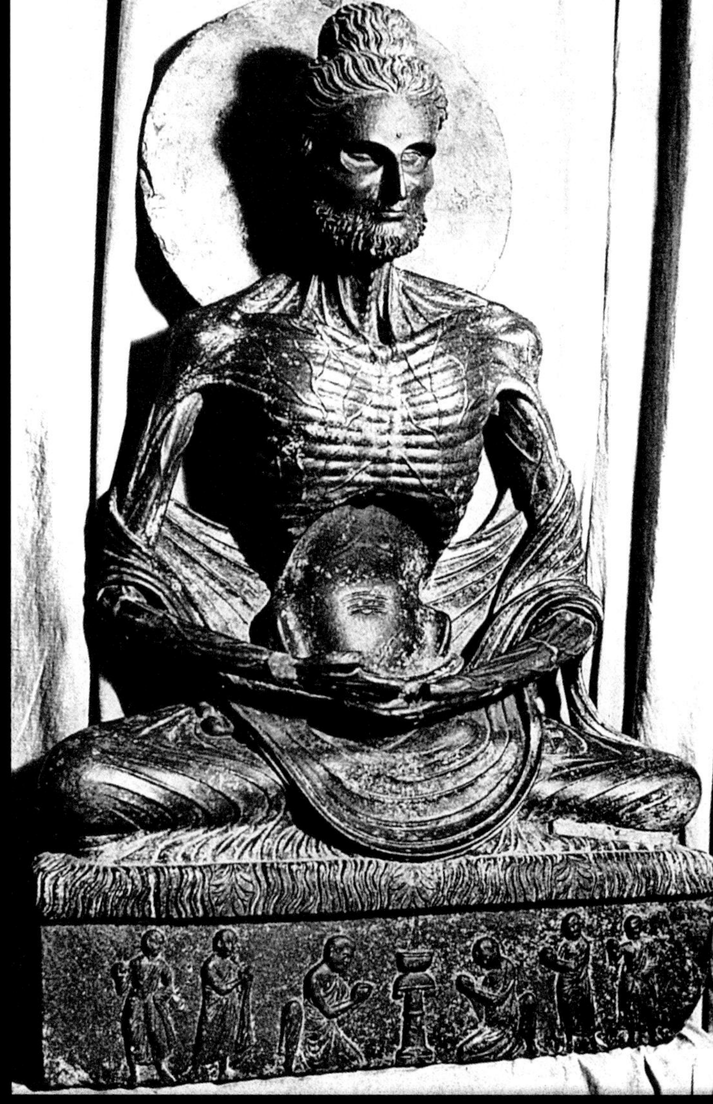

In 460 AD. colossal Buddhist images were begun at Yun-Kang, China. In the sixth century excavations there and at Lung-Men, Tun-Huang, Maichaishan, and other great cave temple sites, the arhat-lohan images were becoming traditional in the buddha pentad: the central Buddha figure flanked by two lohan disciples, usually characterizations of Ananda and Kasyapa, and two Bodhisattvas, with stylized faces, all in clay over rock, with fine color and finish. Some of the disciple faces share characteristics with the I-Chou Lohans.

FASTING SHAKYAMUNI, Gandhara, 1-2nd C AD.

This image represents the period before enlightenment when he realized that his intensive fasting was dwelling in an extreme. He then accepted nourishment in the form of milk and honey offered by a woman. That night Shakyamuni became a Buddha.

It was difficult to convey facial expression with stone relief in Gandhara, but when Chinese sculptors in the cave-temples at Tun-Huang made polychromed clay Lohans, the clay and paint brought a new dimension of expressiveness to the images of the disciples.

In Ch'an legends, the transmission went from Buddha to Kasyapa and then to Ananda. The appearance of Ananda and Kasyapa in the shrines of China is probably due both to Gandharan art traditions and to scriptural reference. Ananda's image, in Gandhara and in China, is of an unlined, youthful face and Kasyapa is given an older and more expressive lined face.

Before the time of Ch'an patriarch Pai Chang (720-814 AD), meditation was taught in buildings called

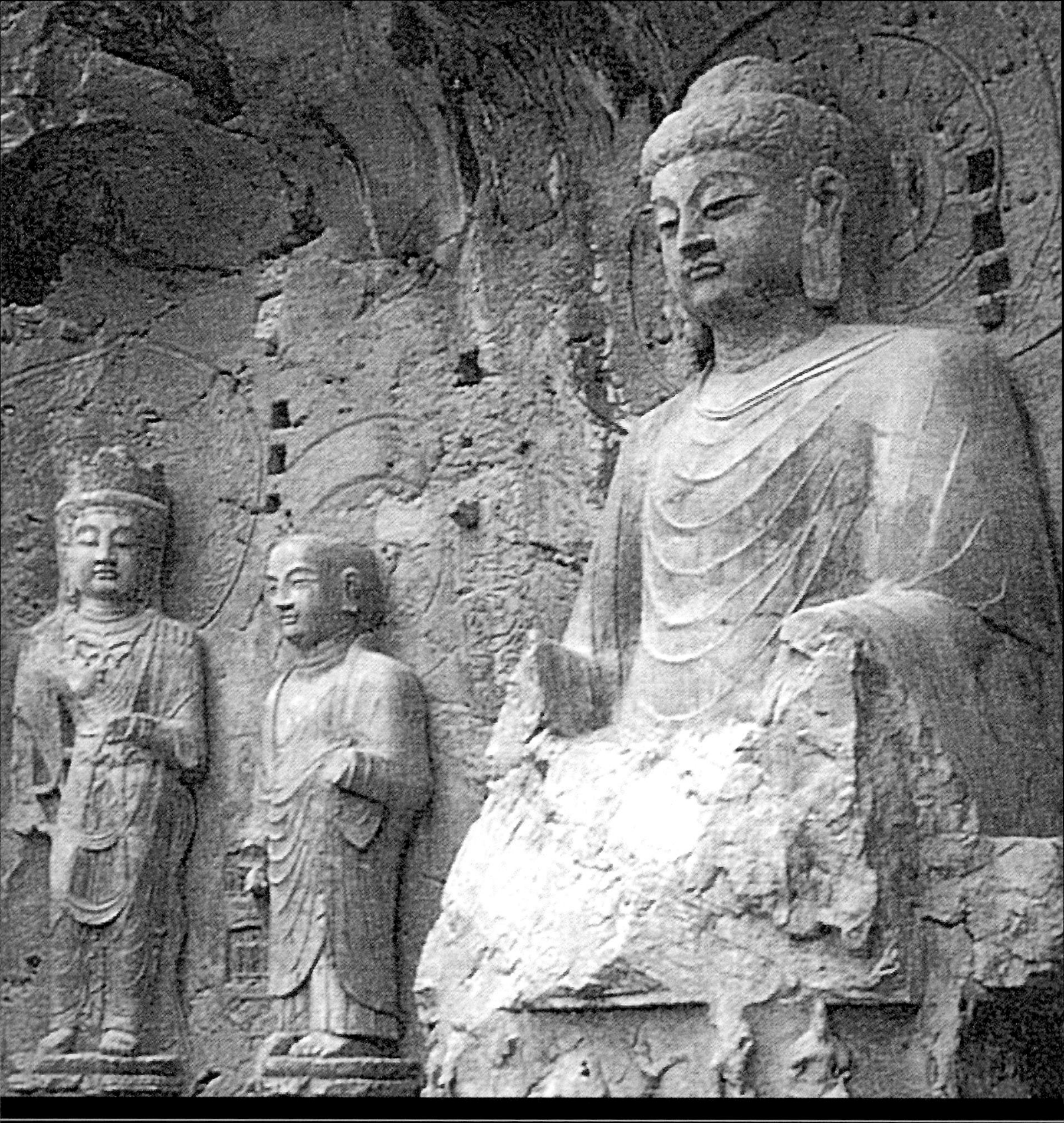

Lung-Men,
China, 7th C AD.

Ananda to the left of the Buddha in the colossal pentad. The colossal Buddha and shrine excavations at Bamiyan Gandhara, on the Silk Route, had a powerful impact on travellers. That impact was carried into China where the Gandharan images were used as models and inspiration.

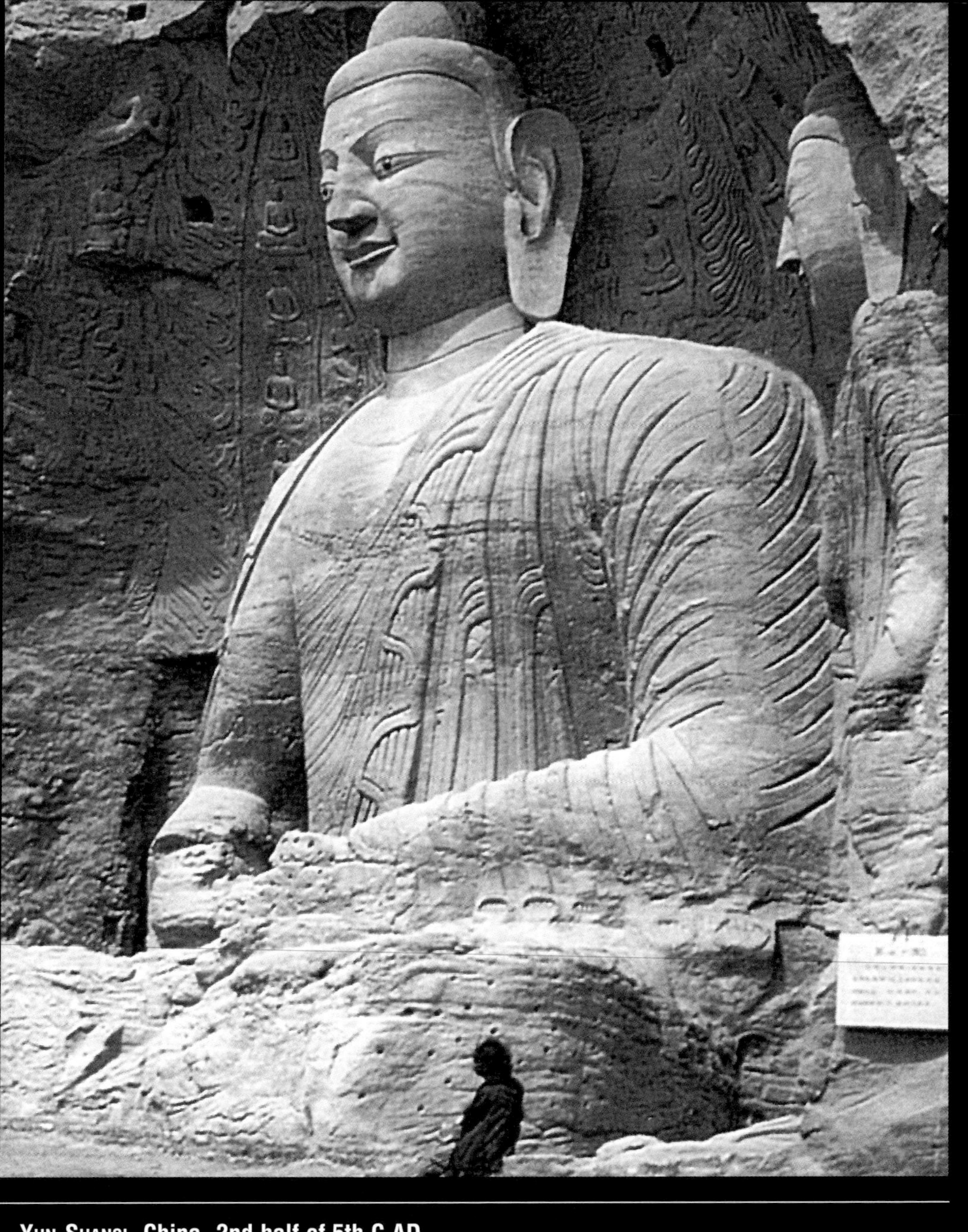

Yun-Shansi, China, 2nd half of 5th C AD.
Colossal Buddha, cave 20, Yun-Shansi. Stone, Height 45'.

Bodhidharma, Chinese porcelain figurine, 18" high. 17th C AD.

Bodhidharma: According to the legends, the Ch'an transmission went from the Buddha to Kasyapa, the First Patriarch, and eventually to Bodhidharma, the 28th Indian Patriarch. Bodhidharma, alone, brought the line into China where it was transmitted to the First Chinese Patriarch. Under the sixth and last patriarch, Ch'an emerged as a prominent school of Mahayana Buddhism in China. Bodhidharma images must have been in most Ch'an monasteries and temples, with portrait statues of teachers and the characterizations of the Buddha's disciples.

"meditation cloisters" which were generally attached to monasteries. The separate existence of the "Meditation Sect" was said to begin with Pai Chang. Special meditation monasteries were built without any buddha halls, but with a gallery containing portrait statues of previous meditation masters. Such statues often had "buddha ears".

The total number of Chinese Buddhist monasteries, large and small, remained essentially the same from the middle of the Sixth Century (30,000 to 40,000) to the end of the Thirteenth Century (some 42,000). The records list some 4,000 as very large monasteries, built through the centuries, with great arrays of art. Some lohan sets must have been made for the atmosphere of living masters. Many were made with reverence for the tradition.

From the original lohan set of the two disciples of the Chinese pentad, Ananda and Kasyapa, the lohans expanded to 16 or 18 during the T'ang Dynasty, sometimes being placed down the sides of the Buddha hall. The shrine was extended to surround the meditators with imagery of meditation.

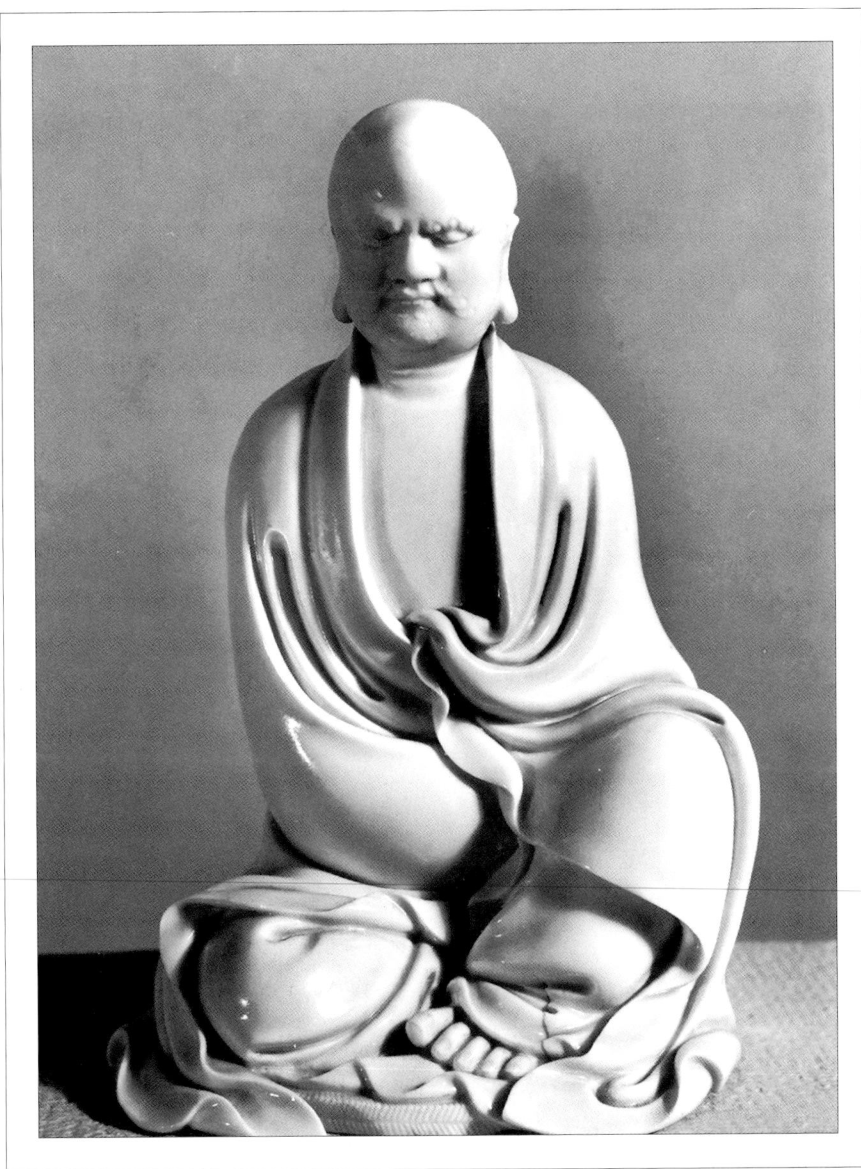

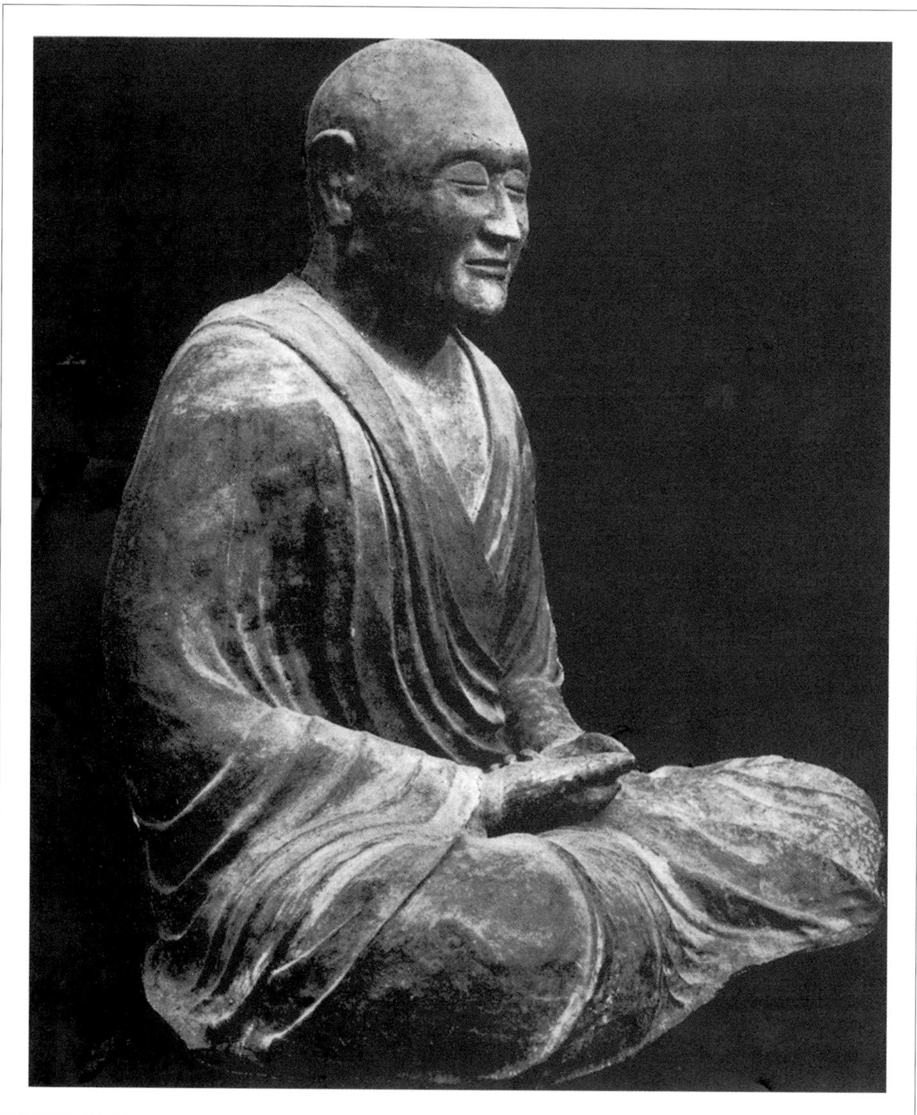

PORTRAIT OF PRIEST GANJIN,
Japanese, from the Kaisando, Toshoda-ji, Nara
Dry Lacquer, height 32,"
Nara period, mid 8th C AD.
Japanese priest portrait sculpture continued the Chinese tradition as Ch'an and other Buddhist lineages were transmitted to Japan.

Gradually the lohan halls in Chinese monasteries become larger and evolved into the "Five Hundred Lohan" halls,[7] some of which still survive, with many Taoist and Chinese cultural and legendary figures included as 'Lohans'.

Comparing the Gandharan "portrait-like" images of monks with the I-Chou Lohans, though more than 800 years apart, they have some identical characteristics. The head is shaved and the body, covered with robes, is often seated in meditation. The structure of the head is shown; the brows are large and there are always the great ears. Line is used in the face to define flesh with contour and expression. But for all these common features of Gandharan and Chinese monk-disciple images, there is a great difference in expressive potential between the best of Gandharan bas-relief monk images and the I-Chou Lohan statues. In Northern Buddhism, the monk-lohan image developed psychological expressiveness, the potential to represent mind and awareness. The imagery began and developed beside the image of the Buddha in meditation in the Gandharan stone reliefs and then became traditional in China, Tibet and Japan. Buddhism went up the Silk Route, slowly and

Stone Buddha Colossus
Polonnaruwa,
Shri Lanka
Ananda standing near the head of the Buddha at his Parinirvana (opposite page)

Priest Eison (Kosho Bosatsu) 13th C AD. Wood with color. Nara. Kamakura period. H. 73.9 cm. Byakugo-ji (below)

powerfully, and Northern nations developed great Buddhist traditions. Disciples of the Buddha were rendered in all art forms. In the sculpture of North Asian cultures there were some masterpiece lohan sets of magnificent quality.

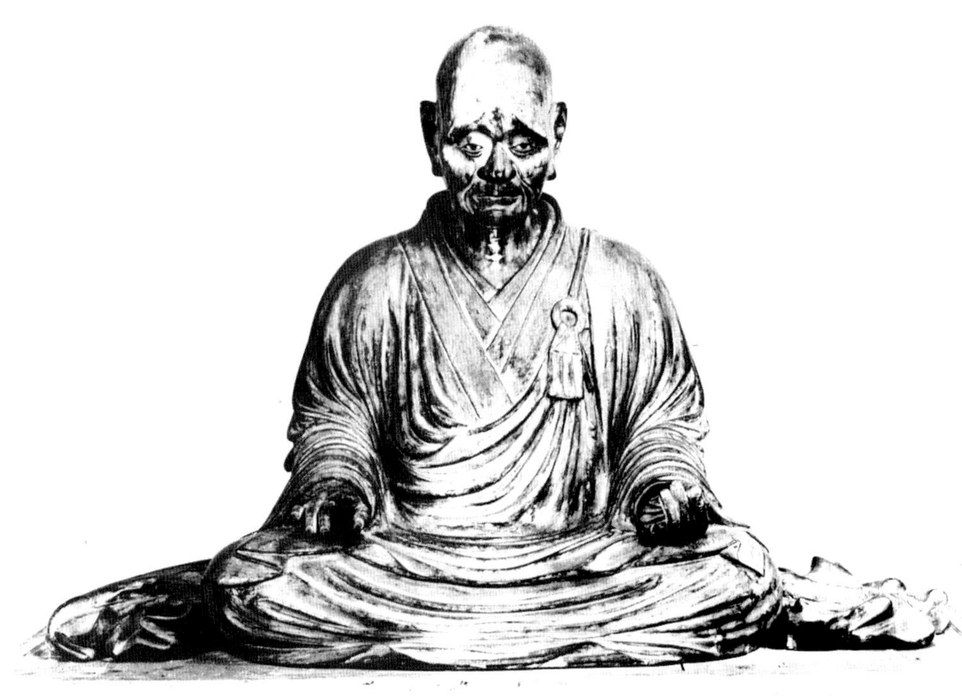

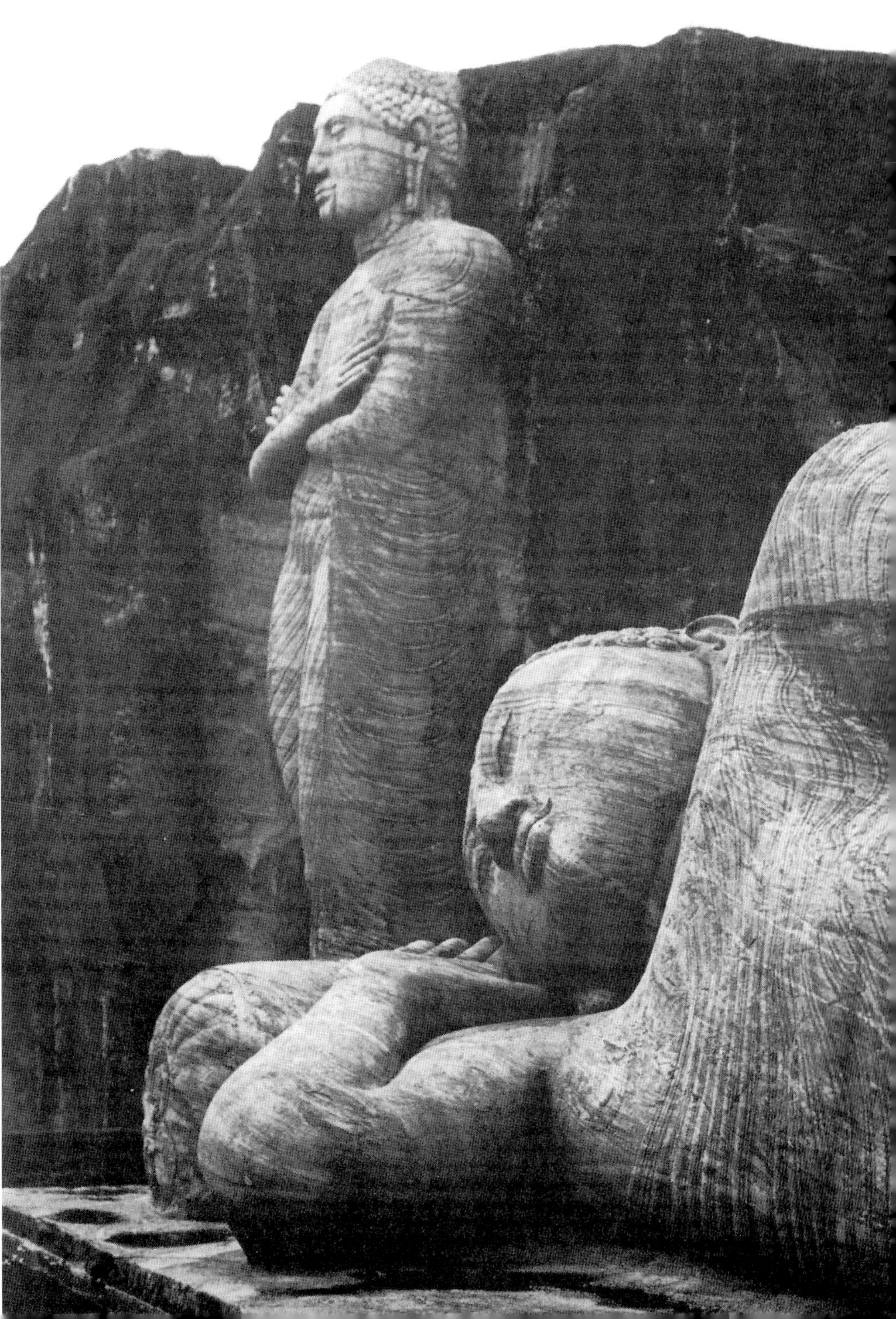

THE DISCIPLES IN THE TIBETAN TRADITION

In Dudjom Rinpoche's unparalleled great work, The Nyingma School Of Tibetan Buddhism, in a chapter called The Patriarchs of The Teaching, Rinpoche says that traditionally 16 great elders or patriarchs have been mentioned, but in his opinion there were "only seven patriarchs before Nagarjuna." (p.437) First there was Mahakasyapa. The Teacher appointed him to be his successor and entrusted the patriarchy to him, but also entrusted it to "the great and exalted Sixteen Elders." Kasyapa compiled the transmitted precepts well and protected the Teaching. For more than 40 years he advanced the Teaching by establishing many disciples on the path of liberation. Kasyapa entrusted the Teaching to Ananda, who was also a direct disciple of the Teacher. Ananda received the essential transmission from Kasyapa through "gradual ordination."

The patriarchy then went from Ananda to Sanavasika, about whom nothing more is said. From Sanavasika the patriarchy went to Upagupta, who had been predicted by the Teacher in the Minor Transmissions as one who will become a Buddha without the marks of one, and will perform the deeds of a Buddha. Through Upagupta's "Seven Instructions" many became arhats. He entrusted the patriarchy to Dhitika. Dhitika entrusted it to Krsna, who in turn entrusted it to Sudarsana, the last of the seven patriarchs of the Teaching before Nagarjuna. Thus these seven are called patriarchs, elders, protectors of the Teaching. But then the Dudjom Rinpoche text says, "In particular, the great Sixteen Elders, who resided with five hundred arhats and others in various lands throughout the four continents and in the Trayatrimsa heaven, protected the precious teaching; and in doing so they visited China during the reigns of T'ang T'ai-tsung, Qubilai Qan, and the emperor Yung-lo. Some say that they could be seen by all, but others maintain that the common folk could not see them, their bodies being rainbow-like." (p.438). And so it was that in Tibet as well as China, traditions of sixteen patriarchs of the Teaching prevailed in scripture and art, with varying identities and attributes. As with the seven patriarchs cited by Dudjom Rinpoche, some of the legendary disciples lived in ages after the lifetime of the Teacher. Yet in the indescribable deathless field of the Awakened One, they were each direct disciples and true patriarchs of the Teaching which is still alive in the present age.

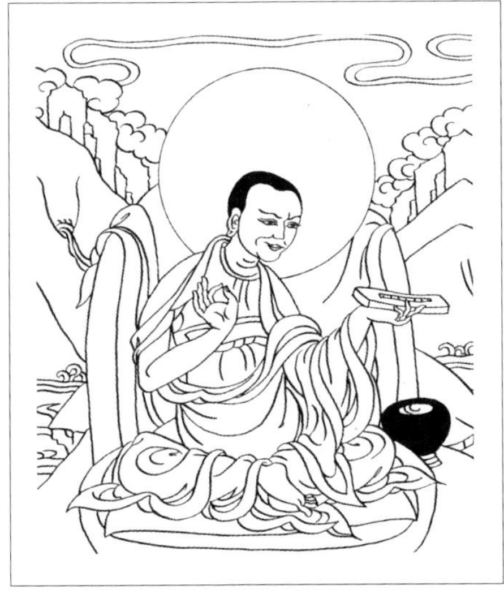

MAHAKASYAPA

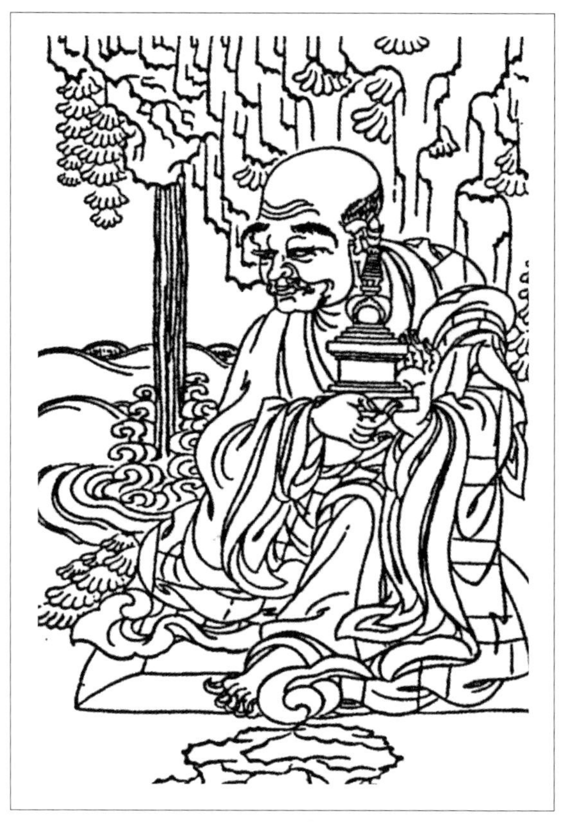

Abheda

The Torch of Precious Jewels:

Sadhana of the Buddha and Sixteen Arhats

by Jigdral Yeshe Dorje
(Dudjom Rinpoche)

Chanteloube, France, 1986

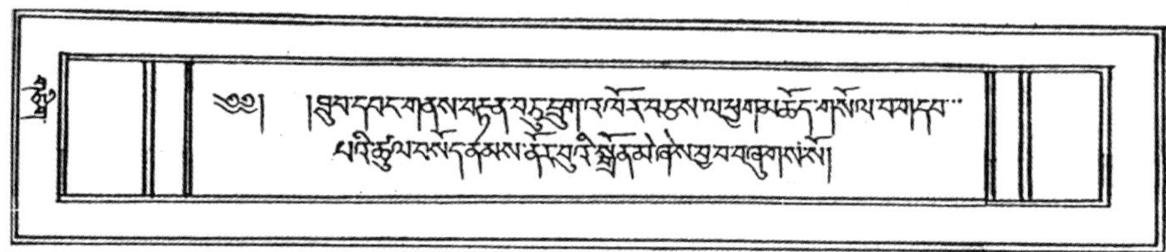

The Torch of Precious Jewels:

a method of obeisance, offering and prayer

to

the Buddha

with the Sixteen Sthaviras and their retinue.

OM SVASTI

Vanquishing the darkness of ignorance of
the Three Worlds[1]
Skillfully he emanates the light of true happiness
and Peace.
Bowing down respectfully to the Mighty One and
his Disciples,
I shall expound clearly and concisely the practice
for accomplishing them.

Those who wish to engage in a method of offering and prayer to the Teacher and Mahasthaviras should, in preparation, sweep and clean a place of purity such as a Vihara and decorate it with ornaments. In the center display the particular supports of the practice, such as images of the Buddha[2] and Mahasthaviras.[3] In front of them, on a clean table sprinkled with the five ingredients from a cow[4] and arrayed with mandalas, cleanly and beautifully arrange whatever articles of offering are available, the two water offerings, the five general offerings[5], and so on. Sit comfortably, in an unwavering state of devotion and excellent motivation.

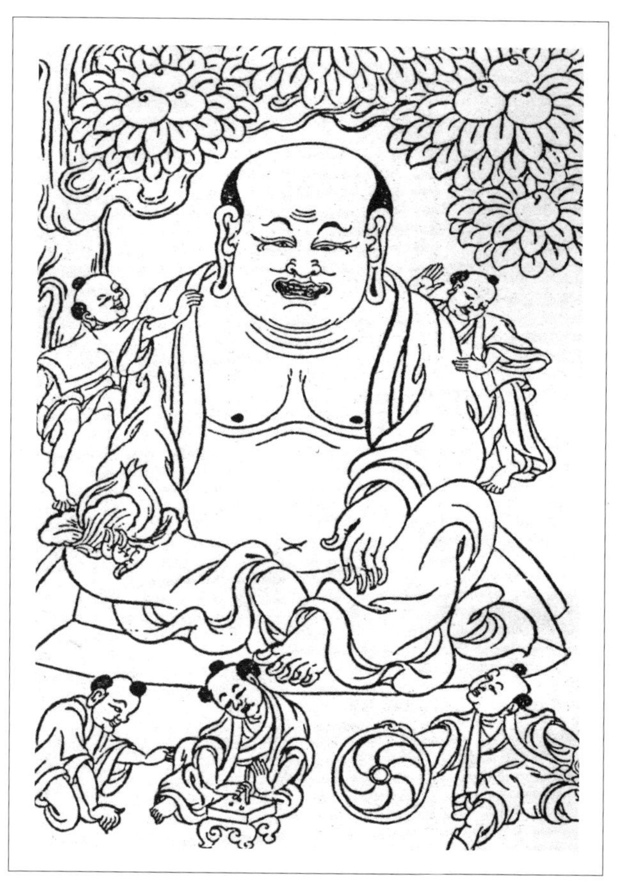

HASHANG

The Preparation

First, the Refuge and the Bodhicitta:
In the Jewels of the Buddha, the Dharma and the Sangha
We take Refuge until we attain Enlightenment.
By the merit of practicing generosity and the like[6]
May we attain Buddhahood for the benefit of beings.

Say this three times.

May all beings come to possess happiness and the cause of happiness.
May they come to be free from suffering and the cause of suffering.
May they never separate from the happiness which is without suffering.
May they come to rest in the Boundless Equanimity which is free from both attachment to loved ones and hatred for others.
Saying this three times, meditate on the four Boundless Wishes[7]

Blessing the place and offerings:

By the Truth of the Three Jewels, the blessings of all the Buddhas and Bodhisattvas, the sovereign might of the two accumulations fully perfected[8] and the power of the inconceivable and utterly pure nature of the Dharmadhatu, now the ground around becomes like the landscape of the Buddhafield of Great Bliss, lavishly decorated with the most perfect ornaments, beautiful, exquisite, inconceivable. May the ground everywhere become soft, the nature of lapis lazuli, even like the palm of the hand, and free from stones.

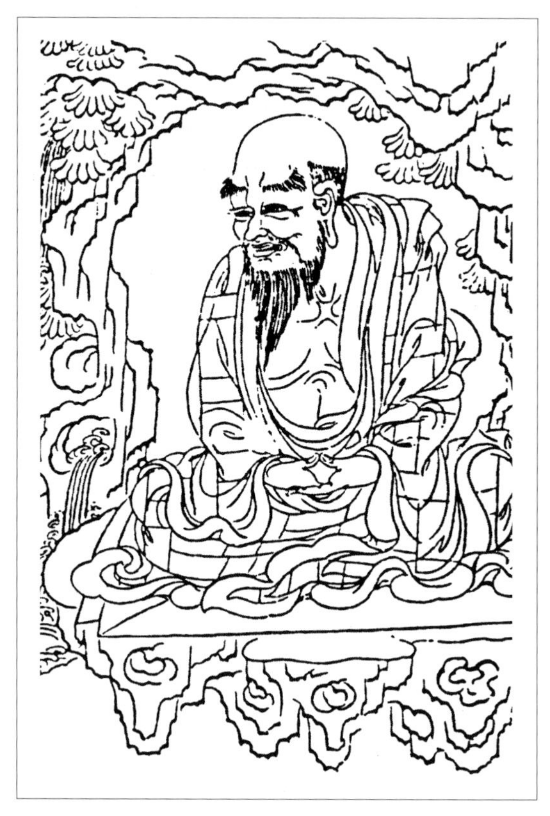

Kanakabharadvaja

In these perfect Buddhafields, the finest possessions of gods and men, forms, sounds, smells, tastes and feelings, perfectly pure, become inconceivable infinite clouds of beautiful offerings filling all space.

As well as these, may there be other offerings, music and melodies pleasing to the ear, clouds existing to dispel the sufferings of beings according to their individual needs:

OM SARWA BITPURA PURA SURA SURA AWARTAYA AWARTAYA HO NAMA SARWA TATHAGATE BHYO BISHO MUKHEBE SARWA THAKHAM UTGATE SAPARANA IMAM GAGANA KHAM SOHA

This is the blessing.

The Main Practice.

The invitation, addressing the object of offering and burning incense:

The ground is even like the palm of the hand, decorated with jewel
ornaments and arrayed with lakes and wish-fulfilling trees.
In the middle is the Measureless Palace, manifested out of jewels, with
four corners.
Upon a seat ornamented with a lotus, sun and moon
Is the Protector of beings, who through compassion establishes on
the path of perfect liberation
Those who are to be benefited in times of strife.
Supreme Buddha and Mahasthaviras, along with your retinues,
we pray, come to this place.
All you Conquerors in the ten directions and your Sons,
you who dry up the ocean of klesas[9] with the blazing fire of Wisdom,
You who, abiding by the Buddha's Teaching, are the field of accumulation
of merit, the source of perfect liberation.
Sanghas of Sravakas in the ten directions, we beseech you to be seated.

Inviting you to this place for a banquet
With these offerings for the sake of beings we pray, come!
Mahasthavira Arhats who open the treasure chest of the Teachings,
The Buddha's Doctrine is in your hands.
By the Protector of beings, lion of the Shakyas,
We beseech you to be seated.

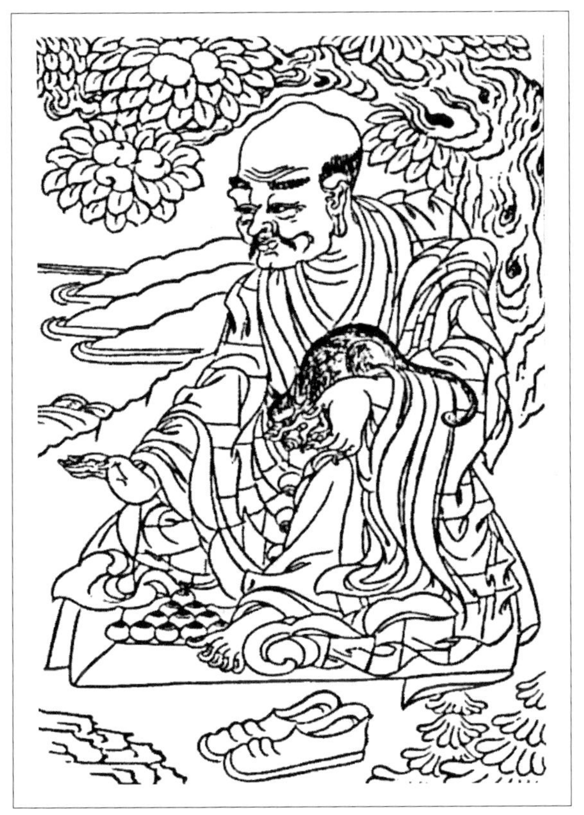

Bakula

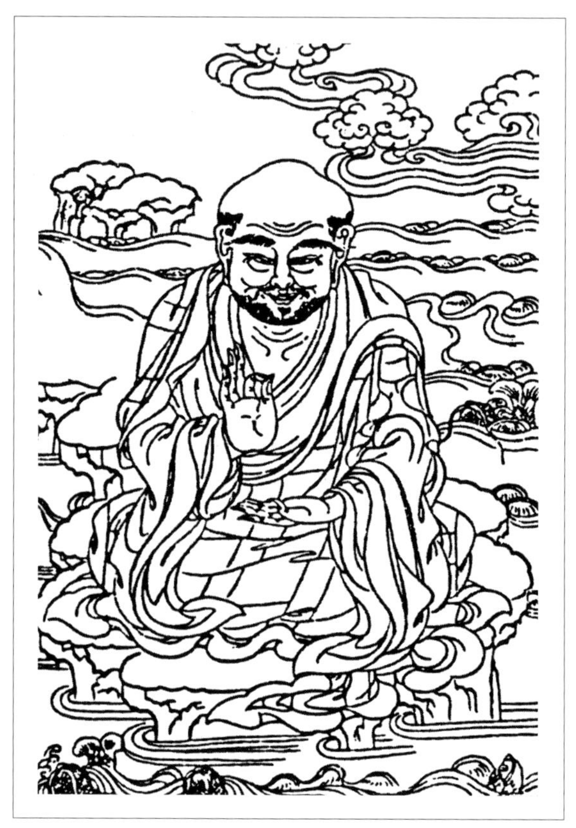

BHADRA

Inviting you in order to spread the holy Dharma,
With these offerings for the sake of beings we pray, come!
You who were instructed by the Buddha to hold the Victory Banner of the Doctrine, ANGAJA, AJITA and VANAVASIN, KALIKA, VAJRIPUTRA and BHADRA, KANAKAVASTA and the sublime KANAKA BHARADVAJA, the exalted BAKULA and RAHULA, CUDAPANTHAKA and PINDOLA BHARADVAJA, PANTHAKA, NAGASENA, GOPAKA and ABHEDA,
With these offerings for the sake of beings we pray, come!

Although you are fully awakened with perfect Wisdom and freedom,[10]
You take the way of the Sravakas according to the faculties of those to be benefited;
Sixteen Sthaviras whose special activity is to protect the Dharma,
Come to this place and take your seat.
You who guard all the Teachings and in particular the Sugata's Teaching and its transmission,
Sixteen Sthaviras who, casting aside your own interests,
Devote yourselves to the good of others in the dense forest of Samsara.
Through the power of your compassion and promises, come to this place.
Praying for the refuge of the Upasaka,[11] listening to words of truth,
Praying that we may be the servants of the Three Jewels
And inviting you to the continent of precious fortune,
With these offerings for the sake of beings we pray, come!

OM SARWA TATHAGATA SAPARI WARA I HYE HI
BENZAR SAMADZA

Making this invitation, play music.

The request to remain:

With the auspicious arrival of the Conqueror
We are blessed with fortune and merit.
As long as our offering lasts
So may the Buddha remain.

PEMA KAMALAYA STAM

The bathing offering:

In very sweetly scented bathing chambers
With fine floors of glittering crystal,
Exquisite pillars of blazing jewels,
And canopies of glowing pearls,
We offer to bathe the Tathagatas and their Sons.
From many jeweled vases
Filled with delightfully scented waters,
To the accompaniment of music and song.
As from the moment of your birth

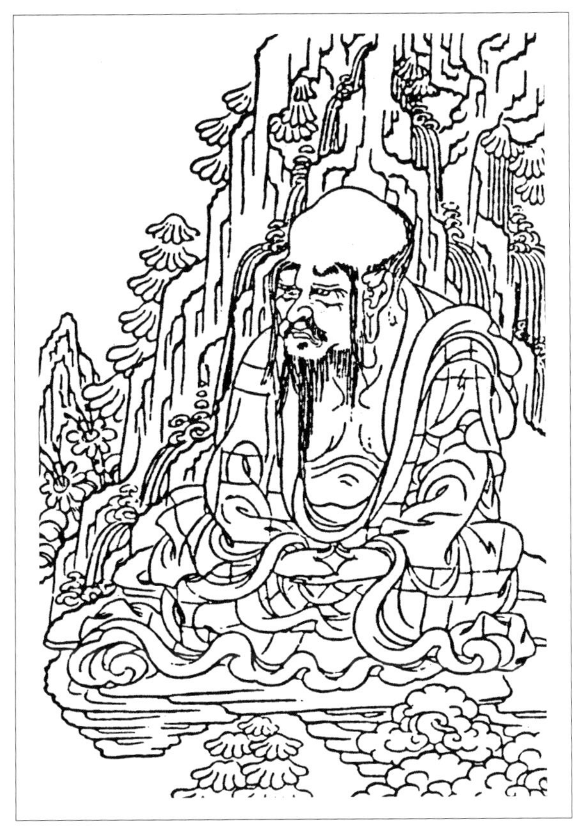

CUDAPANTHAKA

You were bathed by all the celestial beings,
Likewise, with pure celestial waters,
We make the offering of bathing you.
This glorious and sublime ablution
Is the unsurpassable water of Compassion:
Through the blessing with Wisdom water
May you grant accomplishment in accordance with our wishes.

OM SARWA TATHAGATA ABHISHEKATA
SAMAYA SHRI YE HUNG

Drying their bodies:

With the finest cloth, clean and fragrant with the sweetest scents,
We dry your bodies.

OM HUNG TRAM HRI AH KAYA BISHODHANAYA SOHA

The offering of anointing with scent:

With the most exquisite scents
That perfume a thousand million worlds,
As if polishing pure refined gold,
We anoint the blazing, brilliant forms of all the Buddhas.

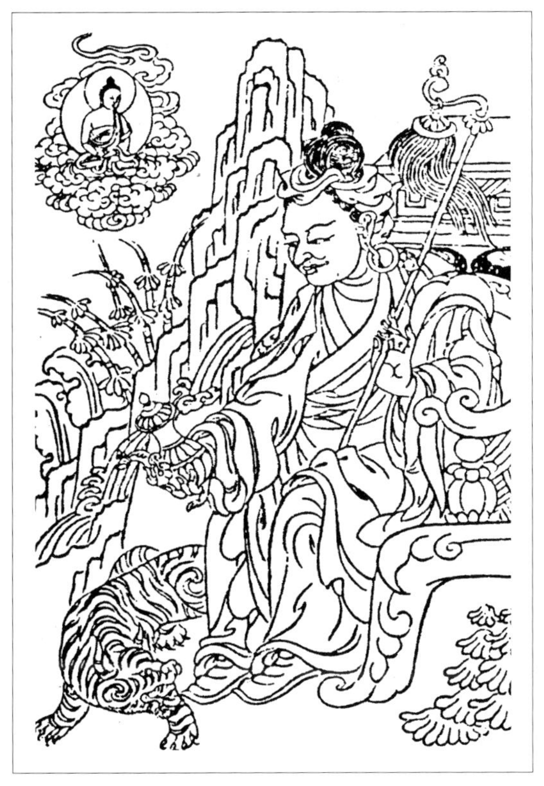

DHARMATALA

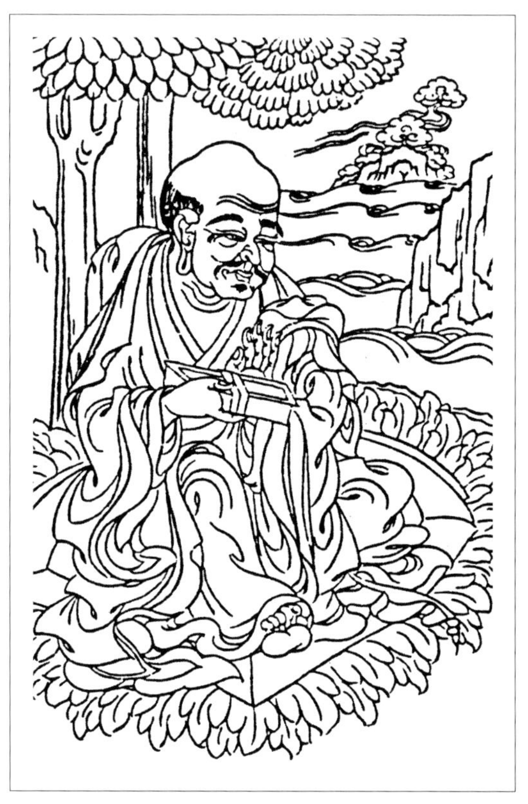

GOPAKA

The offering of raiment:

In order to purify our minds, we make the offering of fine and costly raiment,
Many-colored and splendid as a rainbow
Garments which thrill to touch.
May we be adorned with the clothing of firm patience.

PENTSALIKA PUDZA A HUNG

The accumulation of merit with the Seven Branches[12]

Here, offer the Mandala:

The ground is purified with scented water and strewn with flowers.
It is adorned with Sumeru, the four continents, the sun and moon:
Thinking of it as the blessed Buddhafields, I offer it:
by virtue of this, may all beings here and now attain the
happiness of the Pure Land
IDAM RATNA MANDALA KAM NIRYATAYAMI

and so on, as for the usual Thirty Seven Mandala Offering

Concluding with:

...MATSANGWA MEPA DI NYI NAMDREN TÕNCHOK TUBPE
WONGPO PAKPA NETEN DRACHOM NYENTÕ TENKYONG
GYAMTSOI TSOK DANG CHEPA NAM LA BULWAR GYIO

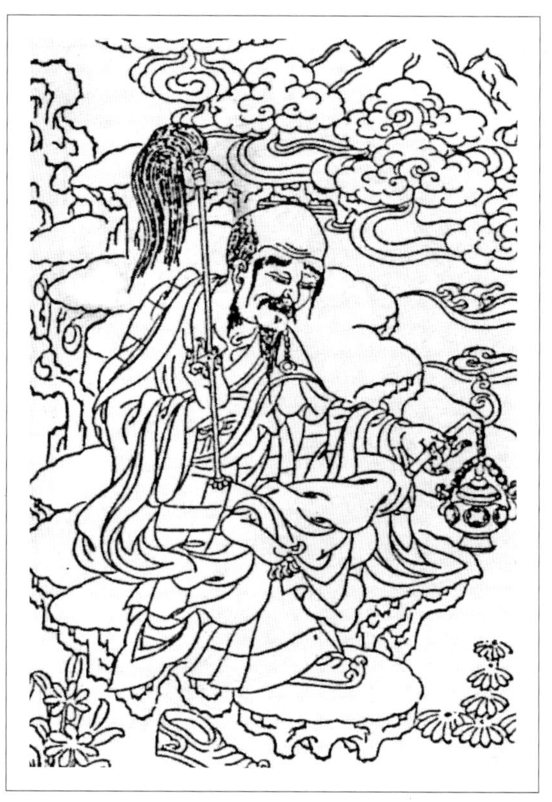

ANGAJA

With nothing lacking all this we offer to the Perfect leader, Supreme Teacher, Mighty Lord, together with the infinite assemblies of Sthaviras, Arhats, Sravakas and Guardians of the Doctrine.
We entreat you, through your compassion accept this offering for the
benefit of beings,
And accepting it, grant blessings, we beseech you

Next, submitting obeisance and
praying for the fulfillment of our wishes:

Unquenchable is the thirst for the sight of him who has no equal:
To him of handsome body and golden hue,
His one face and two hands, sitting in Vajra posture,
In the gestures of Touching the Earth and Equanimity,
we submit obeisance.
For the long life of the Teachers and for the spread of the Teaching,
grant your blessings.

On the great snow mountain of Kailash
Is the exalted STHAVIRA ANGAJA,
Surrounded by one thousand three hundred Arhats:
To him who holds a censer of incense and a yak's tail fly whisk
we submit obeisance.
For the long life of the Teachers and for the spread of the Teaching,
grant your blessings.

On the crystal slopes of the Mountain of Rishis
Is the exalted STHAVIRA AJITA,
Surrounded by one hundred Arhats:
To him who holds his two hands in the mudra of Equanimity
we submit obeisance.
For the long life of the Teachers and for the spread of the Teaching, grant your blessings.

In the Seven Leaves mountain caves
is the exalted STHAVIRA VANAVASIN,
Surrounded by one thousand four hundred Arhats:
To him who threatens with the Pointing Mudra and holds
a yak's tail fly whisk
we submit obeisance.
For the long life of the Teachers and for the spread of the Teaching, grant your blessings.

In the supreme and holy place, the Copper Continent,
Is the exalted STHAVIRA KALIKA,
Surrounded by one thousand one hundred Arhats:
To him who holds golden earrings
we submit obeisance.
For the long life of the Teachers and for the spread of the Teaching, grant your blessings.

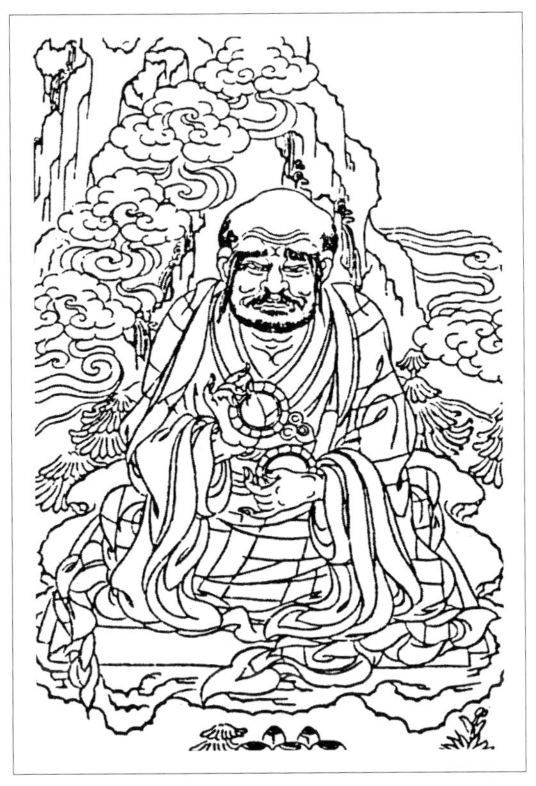

Kalika

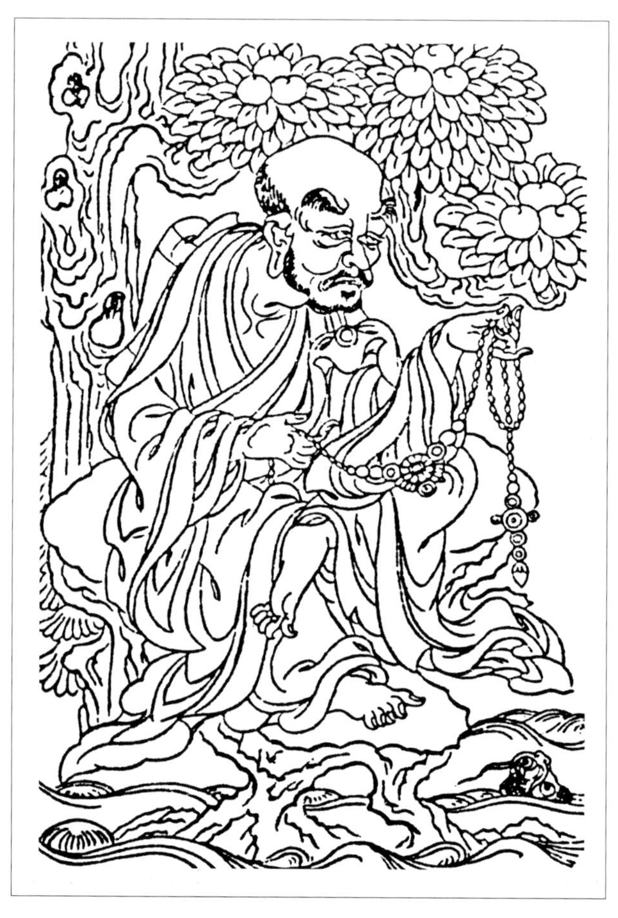

Kanakavasta

On the Lion Island (Shrilanka)
Is the STHAVIRA VAJRIPUTRA,
Surrounded by one thousand Arhats:
To him who threatens with the Pointing Mudra and holds
   a yak's tail fly whisk
      we submit obeisance.
For the long life of the Teachers and for the spread of the Teaching,
grant your blessings.

On an island in the Yamuna River
Is the exalted Sthavira Bhadra,
Surrounded by one thousand two hundred Arhats:
To him who displays the mudras of Expounding the Dharma
   and Equanimity
      we submit obeisance.
For the long life of the Teachers and for the spread of the Teaching,
grant your blessings.

In the supreme and holy place of Kashmir
Is the exalted Sthavira Kanakavasta,
Surrounded by five hundred great Arhats:
To him who holds a jewel lasso
      we submit obeisance.
For the long life of the Teachers and for the spread of the Teaching,
grant your blessings.

In the western continent of Aparogodaniya

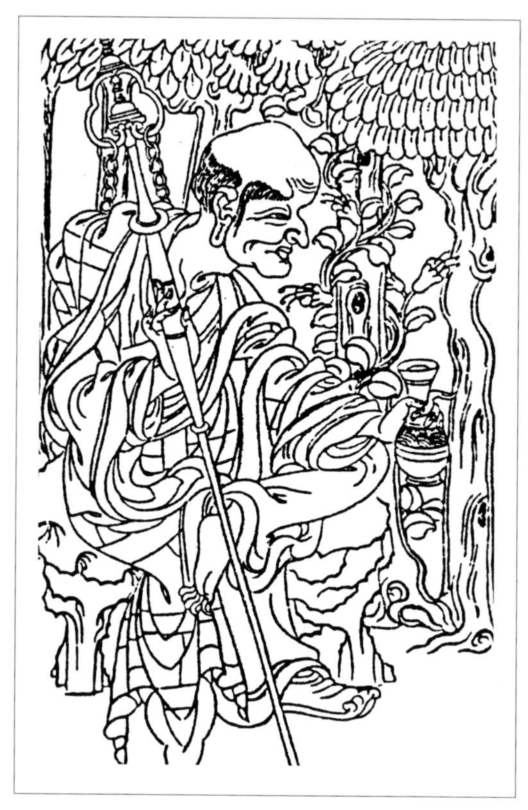

NAGASENA

Is the sublime Kanaka Bharadvaja,
Surrounded by seven hundred great Arhats:
To him who holds his two hands in the mudra of Equanimity
we submit obeisance.
For the long life of the Teachers and for the spread of the Teaching,
grant your blessings.

In the northern continent of Uttarakuru
Is the exalted Sthavira Bakula,
Surrounded by nine hundred great Arhats:
To him who holds in his two hands a jewel-spitting mongoose,
we submit obeisance.
For the long life of the Teachers and for the spread of the Teaching,
grant your blessings.

In the continent of Priyang Gu
Is the exalted Sthavira Rahula,
Surrounded by one thousand one hundred Arhats:
To him who holds a jeweled crown
we submit obeisance.
For the long life of the Teachers and for the spread of the Teaching,
grant your blessings.

On the Vulture Peak
Is the exalted Sthavira Cudapanthaka,
Surrounded by one thousand six hundred Arhats:
To him who holds his two hands in the mudra of Equanimity
we submit obeisance.
For the long life of the Teachers and for the spread of the Teaching,
grant your blessings.

In the eastern continent of Purvavideha
Is the exalted Pindola Bharadvaja,
Surrounded by one thousand Arhats:
To him who holds a book and an alms bowl
we submit obeisance.
For the long life of the Teachers and for the spread of the Teaching,
grant your blessings.

In the realm of the gods, the Thirty Three,
Is the exalted Sthavira Panthaka,
Surrounded by one thousand nine hundred Arhats:
To him who holds a book and displays the mudra of
Expounding the Dharma
we submit obeisance.
For the long life of the Teachers and for the spread of the Teaching,
grant your blessings.

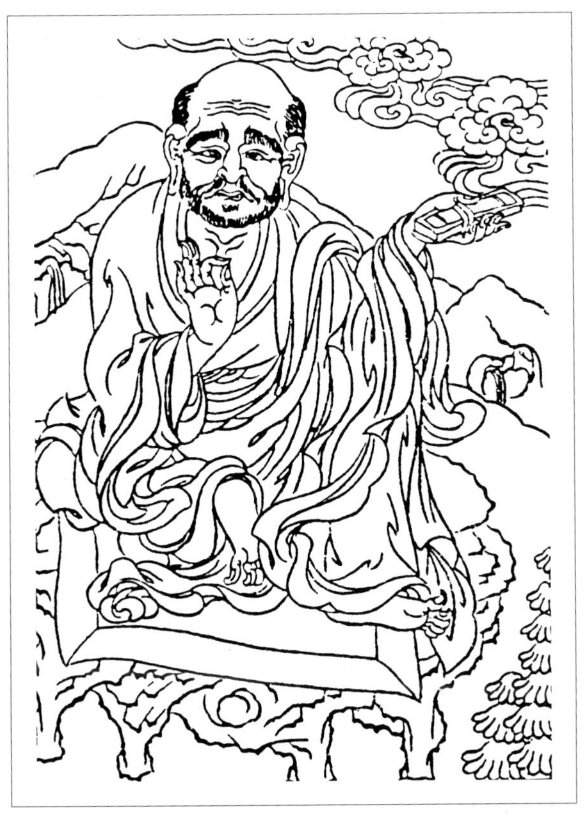

PANTHAKA

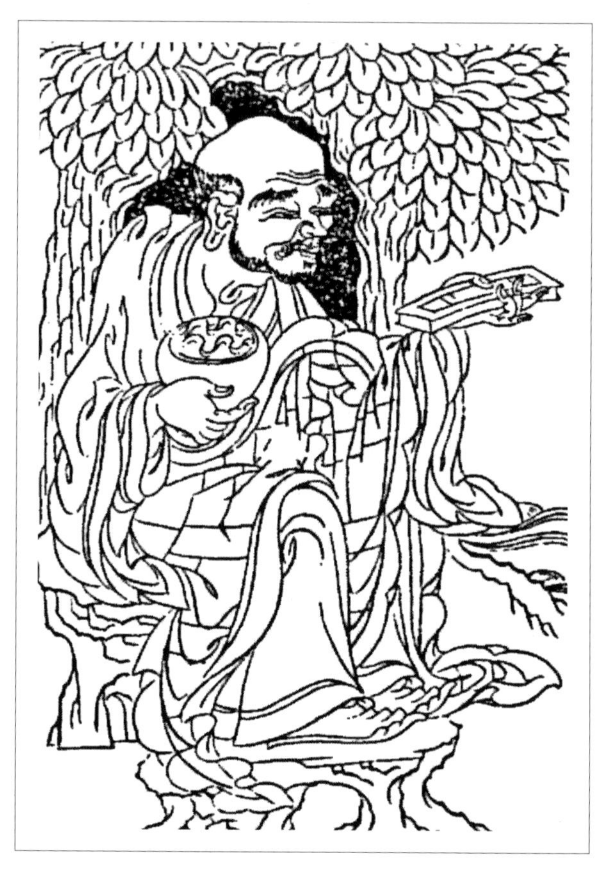

Pindolabharadvaja

On the King of Mountains, Urumundu,
Is the exalted Sthavira Nagasena,
Surrounded by one thousand two hundred Arhats:
To him who holds a vase and a mendicant's staff
we submit obeisance.
For the long life of the Teachers and for the spread of the Teaching,
grant your blessings.

On the King of Mountains, Bihula,
Is the exalted Sthavira Gopaka,
Surrounded by one thousand four hundred Arhats:
To him who holds a book in his two hands
we submit obeisance.
For the long life of the Teachers and for the spread of the Teaching,
grant your blessings.

On the King of Mountains, Himalaya,
Is the exalted Sthavira Abheda,
Surrounded by one thousand Arhats:
To him who holds the Stupa of Great Purity
we submit obeisance.
For the long life of the Teachers and for the spread of the Teaching,
grant your blessings.

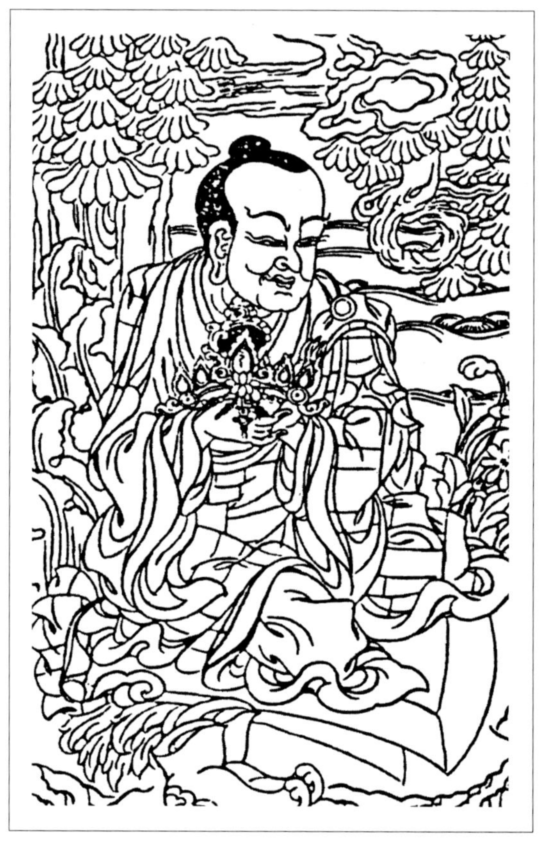

RAHULA

To the exalted Upasaka Dharmatala,
His long hair tied on top, with his load of books,
And Amitabha, the Buddha of Infinite Light, in front,
To him who holds a yak's tail fly whisk and a vase
  we submit obeisance.
For the long life of the Teachers and for the spread of the Teaching,
grant your blessings.

To the Powerful Ones armed with endeavor,
Excellent Guardians of the Buddha's Teaching,
In the East, South, West and North,
To the four Great Kings
  we submit obeisance.
For the long life of the Teachers and for the spread of the Teaching,
grant your blessings.

This is the obeisance and prayer.

The recitations of the mantra, calling the Buddha and his retinue by name and thinking that it invokes their heart promise:

TEYATHA OM MUNI MUNI MAHA MUNI
SHAKYA MUNAYE SOHA

Recite this a hundred times or so, as many as possible.

If one wishes, or there is a need, recite the mantra adding this ending which increases the Sangha or whatever ending is appropriate:

...SARWA SANGHARA PARIPURAKA SOHA

Again, a prayer to fulfill one's wishes:

Great Conqueror, Holder of the Throne (of Vajrasana), think of us.
By the power of hearing, remembering, relating, saluting and making offerings to the sublime names of
The Buddha and assemblies of exalted Sthaviras
May we and others, whatever beings there are,
Pacify all disharmony, both temporary and ultimate,
And greatly increase happiness, virtue, glory and wealth.
Grant the blessing that we may be accepted by a Spiritual Friend of the Supreme Vehicle
And be sustained with the nectar of the Buddha's Teaching.
Through your blessings may we keep pure Discipline,[13] and listen, reflect and meditate;

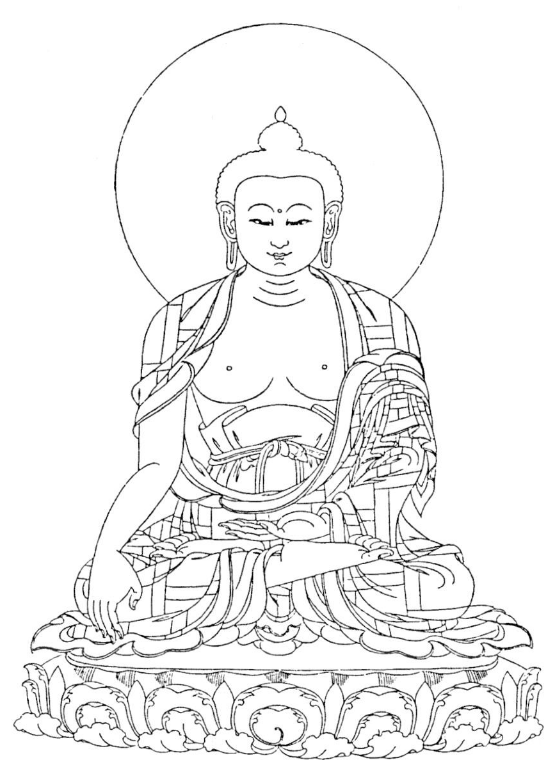

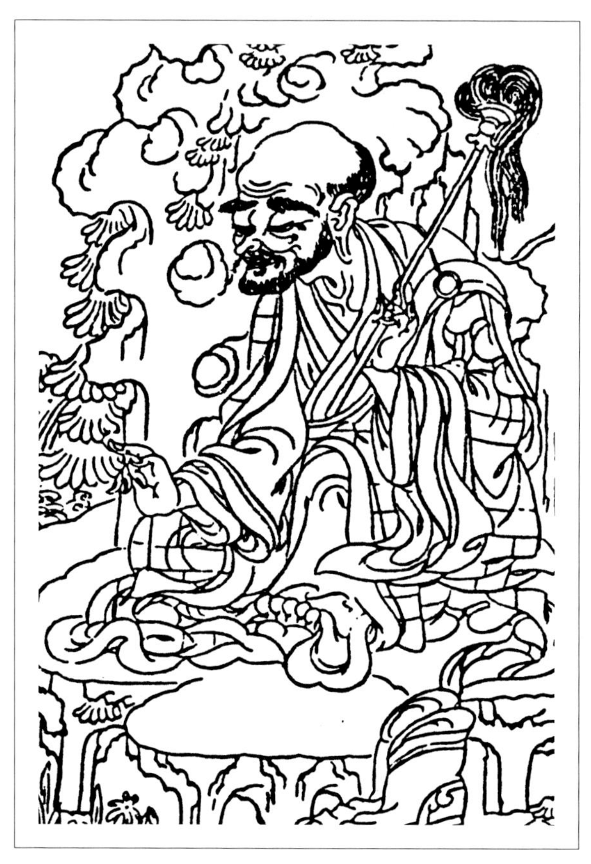

VAJRAPUTRI

May we develop renunciation and train in the two types of Bodhicitta,[14]
Through not being idle in constantly acting for the benefit of others
May we attain the level of Omniscience.
Through your blessings may the stainless doctrine of the Conqueror spread and increase in the ten directions,
May the lives of the sublime holders of the Teaching remain firm for a hundred kalpas,
May the world be filled with great virtue and excellence,
And may the two aims be spontaneously accomplished.[15]
Through your blessings may the ocean of Merit be completed.
May the ocean of Wisdom be perfectly pure.
Having perfected the ocean of qualities, all without exception,
May we become exalted in the Universe.

The Conclusion.

In order to give thanks, offer the Seven Branches as before, or just say this short prayer:

To all you Exalted Beings
We submit obeisance, make offerings and confess our negative actions.
With rejoicing, exhortation and prayer,
We dedicate all our virtue to the Great Enlightenment.
To you who possess the Ten Powers[16] we pray:
Spread the Teaching of the Conqueror;
Remove all obstacles to benefactors,
And purify the defilements of all beings.

Next, in order to make offerings to the four Great Kings, purify the torma with

RAM YAM KHAM,

bless it with

OM AH HUNG,

and offer it by saying the AKARO mantra seven times

OM AKARO MUKHAM SARWA DHARMANAM ATYA NUTPANNA TOTA OM AH HUNG PHAT SOHA

This torma, offered and given[17], possessing the qualities
desirable to the five senses,
We offer to the four Great Kings and others,
To the host of loyal Protectors, guardians of virtue.
Spread the Conqueror's Teaching, increase happiness in the world,
And especially for us and our circle of patrons and beneficiaries,
Dispel all misfortune and unfavorable circumstances.
Bring about favorable conditions in accordance with our wishes,
And help us spontaneously accomplish the two aims.

Then, if one wishes, one may do the Ritual in Three Parts to the Guardians of the Directions and Spirits.

The prayer of forgiveness of faults

Lack of preparation, imperfections
And especially, those things we lacked the ability to do—
whatever mistakes we have made in this practice,
protectors of beings, forgive all these.

A prayer that the Deities remain in the images

Here, inseparable from these images,
may you remain for the duration of Samsara.
Grant freedom from sickness, great long life and power,
and all that is sublime and excellent.

OM SUPRA TISHTHA BENZER YE SOHA

A prayer requesting the Deities to depart
Pray that they may remain firmly.
If there are no images as supports, say

To you who benefit beings we pray,
return to your abodes.

requesting them to depart

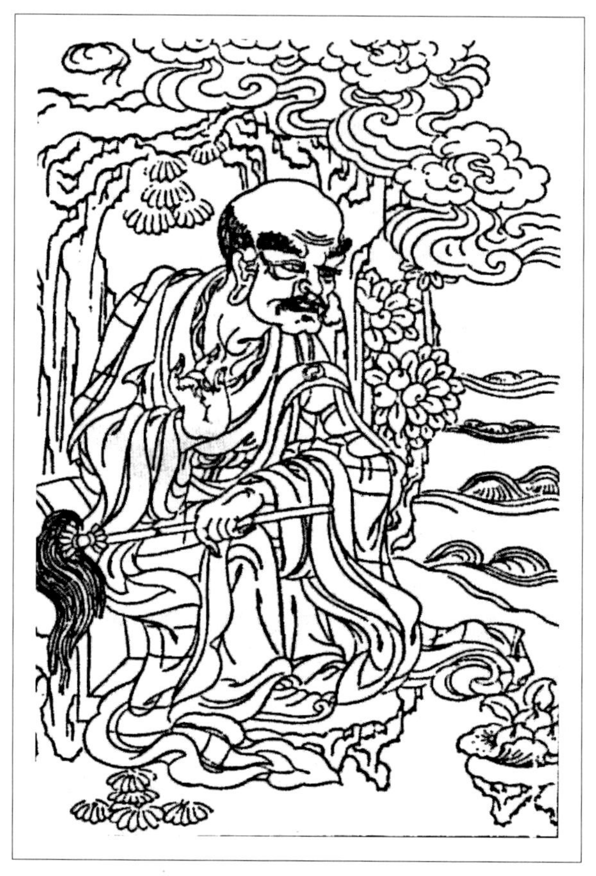

VANAVASIN

The dedication of merit and wishing prayer

By this merit may all beings
Perfect the accumulations of Merit and Wisdom
And attain the two supreme Kayas[18]
Which arise from Merit and Wisdom.
May the Buddha and his host of exalted emanations
Fulfill the activities which protect the Teachings.
Long may the Doctrine remain,
The Teaching of the Mahasthaviras and their retinues.
May there be perfect liberation from Existence, freedom from the klesas.
May birth and death be unknown.
Long may the Doctrine remain,
The Teaching of the Sixteen Thousand Four Hundred.[19]

A prayer for auspiciousness

May the morning be blessed, may the evening be blessed[20]
May the noon as well be blessed,
May the day and night, all the time, be blessed—
Grant this today, Three Jewels.
Glorious teachers, grant this today.
Yidam deities, grant this today.
May the guardians and protectors of the Dharma
And all the local protectors grant us this today.
May all spirits, those gathered here,
On the earth or in space,
Have love for all beings always
And practice virtue day and night.

In this place, by the truth of the Buddha,
The conqueror of all enemies,
Spoken by him as perfectly true,
By that Truth which is free from falsehood,
Today may all be auspicious!
From now on may all be liberated from great fear!

Today all of us practitioners, masters and students,
Together with our circle of patrons and beneficiaries
Be freed from the harmful influences of the sun, moon, planets and
Rahula; may we be completely victorious over all negative forces, faults,
Obstacles and unfavorable circumstances.
May everything be extremely auspiscious!
Victory upon victory!
By the Truth of the Three Jewels,
The blessings of all the Buddhas and Bodhisatvas,
The sovereign might of the the two accumulations perfectly complete
And the power of the inconceivable and utterly pure Dharmadhatu,
May all this be accomplished accordingly.

Through the compassion of the unsurpassable Teacher
And the blessings of the Truth of the Buddhas and Bodhisattvas,
The Pratyekabuddhas and Arhats,
May our dedications and wishes be fulfilled.

Saying this prayer, make wishes.

The benediction,[21] raining down flowers, saying first any suitable auspicious prayers to the Three Jewels.

You who protect the Teaching,
The way of the great Bodhisattvas and Sravakas,
Who unceasingly, for the sake of beings,
Abundantly increase all qualities and virtue.
Mahasthaviras, may all be auspicious!

You who have realized the profound and extensive Teachings,
Dhritarashtra and Virudhaka,
Virupaksha and Vaishravana,
Four Great Kings, may all be auspicious!

May the morning be blessed, may the evening be blessed[22],
May the noon as well be blessed,
May the day and night, all the time, be blessed.
Grant this today, Three Jewels.

Repeating the benediction, make everything auspicious.

Through the merit of making this ritual of offering, praise and prayer
To the Mighty One, Mahasthaviras and their retinues:
May the Buddha's Teaching be expounded and practiced.
May the Doctrine increase and spread.
May all beings be sustained with happiness and peace.

This is how to do, in a condensed way, the well known ritual composed by the great Pandita, Shakya Shri, which combines the obeisance and offering to the Sthaviras.

In accordance with the wish of Tulku Pema Wangyal, who is interested only in holding and propagating the precious Teachings, the Upasaka of the divine race, Jigdrel Yeshe Dorje, compiled this in a restful grass hut in the city of Yambu (Kathmandu), Nepal, on an auspicious day when the moon was waxing in the month of Uttaraphalguni in the year of the Iron Bird (1986). May it become meaningful!

SARWA DA MANGALAM

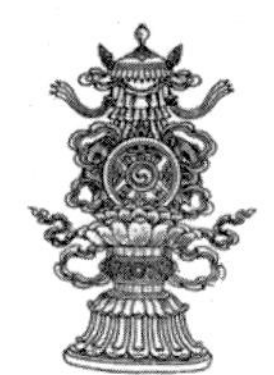

Notes On The Torch Of Precious Jewels

1. The Three Worlds — beneath the earth, the world of nagas;
on the earth, the world of animals and men;
above the earth, the world of gods and asuras.

2. Thub.dbang (Skt. Munindra) — the Mighty Lord or Mighty One.
This and the following terms all signify, and can be translated as, 'Buddha':
Thub.pa (Skt. Muni) — the Mighty One
bCom.ldan (Skt. Bhagawan) — The Conqueror
bCom.ldan. 'das (Skt. Bhagawan) — He who has 'conquered' the klesas, 'possesses' all qualities and has 'gone beyond Samsara'
rGyal.ba (Skt. Jina) — the Victorious One or Conqueror
bDe.gseks (Skt. Sugata) — He who has gone to Bliss
Sangs.rgyas (Skt. buddha) — Buddha.

3. gNas.brtan (Skt. Sthavira)
gNas.brtan.chenpo (Skt. Mahasthavira)
Sthavira means literally 'one who remains firm' and refers to one of the eighteen original schools of the Theravada. Sthaviras were so called because they would remain immovable, with great courage, for long periods of time in places such as caves and forest dwellings. At the same time they had a complete understanding of the Four Noble Truths and thus remained unshakable from that philosophical view.
The Sanskrit term *arhat* means 'one who has conquered all enemies' — that is the klesas or defiling emotions.
'*arhat*' and '*sthavira*' are not synonyms, though a *sthavira* may be an *arhat*, as are indeed the sixteen Sthavira.
The Pali word for Sthavira is 'thera' which has come to have the general meaning of an elder within the Theravaden Sangha.

4. The five ingredients from a cow — the milk, butter, cheese, urine and dung from a red cow born at a particular time, now calved for the first time and milked during a lunar eclipse by a bhiksu who has been ordained for fifteen years with no breach of his vows and who now renews his vows before milking the cow.
These five substances are considered especially pure according to Kriya Tantra.

5. Flower, incense, lamps, scented water and delicacies.

6. The Six Paramitas — generosity, discipline, patience, endeavor, concentration and wisdom

7. The Four Boundless Wishes — loving kindness, compassion, joy and equanimity.

8. The two accumulations — the accumulation of Merit, through virtuous actions such as charity; and the accumulation of Wisdom through the practice of meditation, etc.

9. Nyon.mongs.pa (Skt. Klesa) — the defiling emotions of ignorance, hatred, craving, jealousy and pride.

10. sPang — 'freedom' because they have abandoned (sPang) the klesas.

11. dGe.bsnyen (Skt. Upasaka) — the 'householders' or layman's ordination, normally entailing the observance of five vows: to abstain from killing, stealing, lying, sexual misconduct and the consumption of intoxicants. A prequisite of any of the Buddhist ordinations, of which the Upasaka is the most basic, is to take Refuge in the Three Jewels of the Buddha, the Dharma and Sangha.

12. Seven-Branch Prayer

i.-Homage:

Homage to the greatly compassionate Teacher who,
Making 500 great prayers of aspiration,
Withdrew compassionately from the field of conflict and decadence,
And from whom, once having heard his name, as renowned as the white lotus, one can no longer turn away.

ii.-Offerings:

In imagination I offer, like the Bodhisattva Samanthabhadra,
The clouds of all the physical, verbal, and mental virtuous actions of myself and other beings.

iii.-Confession:

All my errors and failures of Samaya, accumulated throughout beginningless time,
Each and everyone I confess with deep regret.

iv.-Rejoicing:

I rejoice at the virtuous acts of the Aryas and of all human beings,
Accumulated throughout the 3 times.

v.-Request:

I pray you to turn the wheel of the Dharma, wide and deep,
Without interruption in the 10 directions.

vi.-Prayer:

Though in fact, having a wisdom body like space,
You remain in the 3 times without movement or change,
In order to teach in a worldly form, taking birth according to the appearances needed for conversion,
I pray you ever to manifest form-bodies of emanation.

vii.-Dedication:

By the virtuous acts I have accomplished in the 3 times,
In order to be of service to all beings, whose crowd fills space,
To gladden eternally the King of Dharma,
May I attain the level of Lord of Dharma and Conqueror.
Here are the Lady of Charm, the Lady of the Garland,the Lady of Song,
the Lady of Dance, The Lady of Flowers, the Lady of Incense,
the Lady of Perfume.
Here are the Sun and Moon.
Here are the Jeweled Canopy and the Banner ofVictory over the Universe.
The grace, glory, wealth and possession of gods and men, with nothing lacking,

DI NYI TSA WA TANG GYU PAR CHE PEI PEL DEN LA MA TAM PA NAM TANG

All this I offer to the holy Gurus of the Lineage and to the Root Gurus,

YI TAM KYIL KHOR KYI LHA TSHOK SANG GYE TANG CHANG CHUP SEM PEI TSHOK TANG CHE PA NAM LA BUL WAR GYIO

To the Herukas and Divinities of the mandala, and to the assembly of Buddhas and Bodhisattvas.

We entreat the acceptance of this offering through compassion for all beings;
We beseech the bestowal of blessings.

13. Tshul.khrims (Skt. Sila) — discipline (lit. conduct-law), meaning here the observance of pure standards of conduct, precepts and vows which one may have taken according to one's individual capacity.

14. The two types of Bodhicitta — the aspiration to attain Buddhahood for the sake of all beings and the actual practice of the six Paramitas etc. in order to realize that aim.

15. The two aims — the aim of attaining Enlightenment for oneself and that of bringing all other beings to Enlightenment.

16. dBang.bcu — the Ten Powers of a Buddha are defined in general as the ability of a Buddha to accomplish whatever he wishes without impediment or delay.

1. Power over life — the power to remain for a kalpa or longer.
2. Power over the mind — the ability to control at will the entering into and arising out of deep Samadhi.
3. Power over material things — over all material objects.
4. Power over all activities — knowing all the arts and sciences.
5. Power over birth — the ability to take birth wherever he wishes in the six realms.
6. Power over his aspirations — the ability, for example, to fill the thousand million universes with Buddhas and Bodhisattvas.
7. Power of prayer — whatever prayers he may make are accomplished accordingly.
8. Power of miracles — the ability, for example, to accomodate the thousand million universes inside a sesame seed.
9. Power of Wisdom — Having found the Wisdom of all that is to be known.
10. Power of Dharma — the ability to teach all aspects of the Dharma without impediment.

17. mChod.sbyin — offered to the Wisdom Protectors and given to the worldly protectors.

18. The two Kayas — Dharmakaya and Rupakaya, the latter comprising the Sambhogakaya and Nirmanakaya.

19. The Sixteen Sthaviras and their retinues of Arhats.

20. Sis.brjod — benediction or prayer for auspiciousness.

21. bDe.legs — 'blessed' in the sense of auspicious.

Glossary

ABHIJNA (ABHIÑÑÄ) (Skt.): Supernatural knowledge or insight possessed by a Buddha and those who have reached advanced stages of spiritual development. Unlimited knowledge of the universe and sentient beings.

ARHAT (ARHANT) (Skt.): "Worthy", (worthy of offerings). The arhat has extinguished the patterns of thought and emotion leading into samsara. Arhat realization is the fourth and final result of the Hinayana path ("no-more learning"). Also, the direct disciples of the Buddha.

BHUMI (Skt): The ten levels or stages of the Bodhisattva path: the Joyous; the Stainless; the Radiant; the Brilliant; the Hard to Conquer; the Realized; the Reaching Far; the Unshakable; the Good Intelligence; and the Cloud of Dharma.

BODHISATTVA (Skt.): Someone who has developed bodhicitta, the aspiration to attain enlightenment in order to benefit all sentient beings. A practitioner of the Mahayana path, especially one who has attained the First Bhumi.

BUDDHA (Skt.): Enlightened or Awakened One, who has completely abandoned all obscurations and perfected every good quality, all the powerful facilities of the human potential.

BUDDHAMIND: Inherent open awareness, primordial unconditioned wisdom.

BUDDHANATURE: The enlightened essence. Inherently present in all sentient beings. Human beings are capable of realizing it.

CH'AN (Ch.) = Zen (Ja.): The school of Buddhism developed in China with transmission brought from India by Bodhidharma in 520 AD and later brought to Japan. The tradition emphasizes sitting meditation as a means of awakening. Bodhidharma is said to have stayed seated in meditation posture for 9 years facing a wall. It is the essence of renunciation, world and mind, to become aware.

DAKINI (Skt.; Tib., Khandro; literally "sky goer." "sky dancer"): The Feminine aspect of pristine awareness; spiritual beings who fulfill the enlightened activities.

DHARMA (Skt.): The Buddha's teachings. Sacred law. Can also mean phenomena or mental objects.

DZOG CHEN (Tb.): Natural Great Perfection. The ultimate teaching of the Buddha, the direct realization of primordial buddhahood. The supreme teaching of Tibetan Vajrayana buddhism.

FOUR NOBLE TRUTHS: The first teaching given by Sakyamuni Buddha. It is essential Buddhadharma. Beginning with the recognition of pain, confusion, the path to transcendence of pain/confusion is established.

GANDHARA: The historical Northwest Region, northwest of India, from the Indus river extending into modern Afghanistan and Pakistan. Alexander the Great established Hellenic civilization there and the combination of eastern and western influences gave rise to the development of Buddhist art in the 1st and 2nd C AD. The region was an important center for the development of Mahayana Buddhism. Later, in the 9th C AD., the great Vajrayana master Padmasambhava is said to have been born there, in Odiyan or Orgyen, which is associated with the Swat Valley. He is considered to be "the Second Buddha", the one who brought the dynamic practices and teachings of the Vajrayana to Tibet.

HERUKA: (skt.) Literally, 'blood drinker'. Energetic deity nature that drinks the blood of ego clinging.

HINAYANA: Buddhist trainings focused on contemplation of the Four Noble Truths and the 12 links of dependent origination for the sake of personal (individual) liberation.

KUSHANS: A royal blood line devoted to Buddhism, who were associated with the Gandharan region and the Buddhist developments there until the invasion of the White Huns in 461 AD.

MAHASIDDHA (Skt.): Enlightened masters of the Buddhist tantric tradition, beings with magical actions, Indian yogins through whom the Vajrayana was brought to Tibet after Padmasambhava's time.

MAHAMUDRA (Skt.): The Great Symbol, or Sign. This is meditative experience developed through the New Translation school of Vajrayana Buddhism in which the phenomenal world is seen as an expression of fundamental being.

MAHAYANA (Skt.): "The Great Vehicle"' developed in the Buddhist church in the 1st-2nd C AD, in which the Boddhisattva ideal, universal compassion, was established as the heart of the path to enlightenment.

NIRVANA: The extinguishing of the causes for samsaric existence. The lesser nirvana refers to the liberation from cyclic existence attained by a Hinayana practitioner. Greater nirvana refers to the state of enlightenment that falls neither into the extreme of samsaric existence nor into the passive state of cessation attained by an arhat.

PAI-CHANG (749 - 814 AD): Developer of the monastic rules regulating the life of Ch'an monks. The main precepts were meditation and manual labor. "A day without work, a day without eating." Pai-Chang set the example. The rules regulated the arrangement of monastery buildings, the hierarchy of offices and the practice program.

PALI CANON: The scriptures of the Theravada school of Buddhism, in part at least written down in Pali in Celon in the 1st C BC. It is in 3 divisions or "baskets" (Pitaka): The Vinaya or rules of the order; the Sutras or sermons; and the Abhidharma, "beyond Dharma", a collection of teachings concerned with the development of cognitive faculities.

PARINIRVANA: Completly passing beyond suffering. The final entry intoNirvana. Also, an honorific term for the passing away of a buddha or a fully accomplished master.

PENTAD: A group of five figures in buddhist shrine art: a buddha image flanked by four figures, usually a disciple and a bodhisattva on each side of the buddha.

PRAJNA: Superknowledge; the sharp two-edged sword that cuts through all confusion.

SHAKYAMUNI: The sage of the Sakya clan. Buddha Sakyamuni (563-483 BC). The historical Buddha. Divine Incarnate Teacher. The Buddha of our era.

SAMADHI: Adhering to undistracted awareness. Usually translated as concentration or meditative absorption.

SAMSARA: Cyclic existence, vicious circle or round of birth and death and rebirth within the 6 realms of existence characterized by suffering, impermanence and ignorance.

SHAMATHA (Skt.): Calm Abiding. The meditation practice of calming down and staying calm in order to rest free of the disturbances of thought. Various concentration techniques are used, primarily following the breath.

SHUNYATA (Skt.): In the Hinayana, shunyata refers to the lack of a personal ego. From the Mahayana point of view, it means the essentially empty quality of everything. In other sutras it means the brilliant light nature. In Dzogchen it means the primal, pure, fundamental nature. (Thinley Norbu Rinpoche)

SIDDHI (Skt.): Accomplishment. The attainment resulting from meditation practice. There are, traditionally, 8 common siddhis, 8 mundane accomplishments, such as clairvoyance, clairaudience, flying in the sky, becoming invisible, everlasting youth, and powers of transmutation (the ability to control the body and the external world). The most eminent attainments on the path, however, are renunciation, compassion, unshakable faith and realization of the correct view. The supreme siddhi is complete enlightenment.

SILK ROUTE: The road from Rome to China (East - West), through Central Asia, led through several thousand miles of dreary and forbidden regions. Traversing parts of Mongolia and Turkestan, the route included the huge Gobi Desert and Pamin Plateau, "the Roof of the World." The initiative in opening the Silk Route came from both ends about 1st C AD.

STUPA (Skt.): A monument containing relics, the structure of which is both the body of the universe and the symbolic form of the Buddhist path.

THERAVADAN BUDDHISM: One of the major original schools of Buddhism, associated with S.E. Asia, and sometimes associated with Hinayana Buddhism, the "Narrow Path", the "Lesser Vehicle".

TRIAD: A buddha image flanked by two figures, most often either disciples or bodhisattvas.

TRIPITAKA (Skt.): see Pali Canon.

UPEKHA (Skt.) (UPEKKHA, Pali): Equanimity. Serenity. The 4th of the Brahma Viharas and their synthesis, the state of mind in which the other three can be practiced without attachment. A neutral state. Samadhi.

VAJRAYANA (Skt.): The Tibetan Buddhist School. The Diamond Vehicle. The practices of taking the result as the path. Same as Secret Mantra Path or Tantrayana.

VIDYA (Skt): Knowledge. Vidyadhara is knowledge-holder, knowledge-bearer.

VIHARA (Skt): Buddhist or Jain. Monastery or temple; originally a hall where monks met or walked about.

VIMOKSHA: (Skt.) Liberation.

VIPASHYANA (Skt.): Clear or wider seeing. "Panoramic Awareness"; "extraordinary insight". Usually refers to "emptiness", wisdom mind arising from Shamatha practice.

ZAZEN (Ja.): literally "sitting meditation". The primary practice of Ch'an-Zen Buddhism.

Selected Bibliography

Akiyama & Matsubara, **Arts of China, Buddhist Cave Temples,** Kodansha International, Palo Alto, CA, 1969

Blofeld, John, **The Zen Teachings of Hui Hai on Sudden Illumination,** Samuel Weiser & Co., 1962

Bosch Reitz, S.C., **A Large Pottery Lohan of the T'ang Record,** The Metropolitan Museum of Art Bulletin, Jan,1921

Bosch Reitz, S.C., **A Second Pottery Lohan in the Metropolitan Museum of Art,** The Metropolitan Museum of Art Bulletin, June, 1921

Chang Chung-Yuan, **Original Teachings of Ch'an Buddhism,** Vintage Books, Random House, NY, 1971

Chokyi Nyima Rinpoche, **The Union of Mahamudra and Dzogchen,** Rangjung Yeshe Publications, Hong Kong, 1986

Cohn, Wm, **Chinese Painting,** Phaidon Press LTD, 1948

Coomaraswamy, A.D., **Figures of Speech, Figures of Thought,** Luzak and Co., London, 1946

Coomaraswamy, A.D., **Elements of Buddhist Iconography,** Harvard University Press, Cambridge, MA, 1935

DeVisser, Mariss Willem, **The Arhats in China and Japan, #1,** Oesterheld & Co., Berlin, 1923

Dumoulin, Heinrich, **A History of Zen Buddhism,** Beacon Press, Boston, MA, 1969

Fisher, Robert E., **Buddhist Art and Architecture,** Thames and Hudson, London, 1993

Fong, Wen, **The Lohans and a Bridge to Heaven,** Washington, DC, 1958

Glaser, Curt, **Ostasiatische Plastic,** Berlin, 1928

Gyatrul Rinpoche, **Ancient Wisdom,**
Snow Lion Publications, Ithaca, NY, 1993

Hobson, R.L., **Chinese Art,** The Macmillian Co., NY, 1920

The Burlington Magazine, Number XXV,
A New Chinese Masterpiece in the British Museum, 1914

Hopkirk, Peter, Foreign Devils on the Silk Road; **The Seach for the Lost Cities and Treasures of Chinese Central Asia,** John Murray, London, 1970

Inghalt, **Gandharan Art in Pakistan,** Pantheon Books, NY, 1957

Ishigami, Zenno, **Disciples of the Buddha,** Kosei Publishing Co., Tokyo, 1989

Jigdrel Yeshe Dorje, Dudjom Rinpoche, **The Nyingma School of Tibetan Buddhism,** Wisdom Publications, Boston, MA, 1991, 2 Volumes

Lee, Sherman E., **A History of Far Eastern Art,** Harry N. Abrams, NY, 1982

Marshall, Sir John, **The Buddhist Art of Gandhara**, Cambridge University Press, Cambridge England, 1960

McRai, J.R., **The Northern School and the Formation of Early Ch'an Buddhism,** University of Hawaii Press, Honolulu, 1986

Mitra, D., **Buddhist Monuments**, Sahitya Samsad, Calcutta, 1971

Namkhai Norbu Rinpoche, **Primordial Experience**, Shambala Publications, Inc, Boston, MA 1983

Priest, Alan, **Chinese Sculpture In the Metropolitan Museum of Art**, Metropolitan Museum of Art Bulletin, NY, 1944

Prip-Moller, Johannes, **Chinese Buddhist Monasteries**, U. of Hong Kong Press, Hong Kong, 1967

Reischauer, E.O., **Ennin's Travels In T'ang China**, Ronald Press Co., NY 1955

Rowland, Benjamin, **The Art and Architecture of India**, Penguin Books, London, 1953

Sickman, Lawrence & Soper, Alexander, **Art and Architecture of China**, Pelican History of Art, 1956

Shan Shik Buddhist Institute, **The 16 Arhats and the 18 Arhats,** Peking, 1961

Siren, Osvald, **A History of Early Chinese Art**, E. Benn, Ltd., London, 1929

Siren, Osvald, **Chinese Sculpture**, Hacker Art Books, NY, 1970

Speiser, Weiner, **The Art of China**, Spirit and Society, Crown Publishers, NY, 1961

Stein, Sir Auriel, **Innermost Asia**, The Clarendon Press, Oxford, 1928

Sullivan, Michael, **The Arts of China,** University of California Press, Berekley, CA, 1967, 1979

Suzuki, D.T., **An Introduction to Zen Buddhism**, Harper and Row, NY, 1949; — **Essays on Zen Buddhism**, First Series, Harper and Row, NY, 1949; Second Series, Beacon Press, Boston, MA, 1952;
— **Zen Buddhism**, edited by Wm Barrett, Doubleday & Co, NY, 1956

Swann, Peter C., **Chinese Monumental Art**, Viking Press, NY, 1963

Tsukamoto, Zenryu, **A History of Early Chinese Buddhism**, Kodansha Int'l., LTD, Tokyo, NY, SF, 1979

Thinley Norbu Rinpoche, **The Small Golden Key**, Jewel Publishing House, NY, 1977

Trungpa, Chogyam, **Journey Without Goal**, Shambala Publications, Boston, MA, 1981;
— **Cutting through Spiritual Materialism**, Shambala Publications, Boston, MA, 1973;
— **The Myth of Freedom**, Shambala Publications, Boston, 1974,

— **Shambala Sacred Path of the Warrior,** Shambala Publications, Boston,

— **Great Eastern Sun,** Shambala Publications, Boston.

Tulku Thondrup Rinpoche, **Buddha Mind**, Snow Lion Publications, Ithaca, NY, 1989;

— **Enlightened Living,** Rangjung Yeshe Publications, 1990

— **The Practice of Dzogchen,** Snow Lion Publications, 1989

Watters, Thomas, **The 13 Lohan of Chinese Buddhist Temples**, Kelly & Walsh, Shanghai, 1925

Wolfe, Marion, **The Lohans From I-Chou**, Oriental Art, Vol XV

Data

Title of Work of Art:	Disciples of the Buddha; Lohans
Number of Statues	There were probably 16 or 18 statues in the complete work of art.
Artist:	Unknown.
Material:	Ceramic. A gray clay was used to build the substance and form of the statue. It is coated with a layer of fine white slip clay about one-quarter inch thick. The heads are formed of a reddish clay covered with a carefully applied white slip clay. The heads have been fired upside down.
Glaze:	Tri-colored glaze: ivory white, orange gold, and green. The pupils of the eyes are painted in with a fine brown-black clay mixture.
Date of Origin:	9th century, as dated by the Metropolitan Museum, New York City; 10-12th century as dated by others.
Place of Origin:	China, probably within one hundred miles of I-Chou, Chi-Li Province, south of Beiging [PeiKing] where most of the statues were safeguarded in a cave for an unknown period of time. A tablet in the cave read, "ALL THESE BUDDHAS COME FROM FAR AWAY". Even if they were moved more than once, 100 miles was far.
Height:	The statues average about 50 inches in height.
The Bases:	Each of the surviving I-Chou Lohans comes on an individual base. The relatively square structures, about nine inches high, have a green flat surface that supports the flat-bottomed statues. The tri-colored robes of the image seem to flow

into the tri-colored bases. There are complex openings within the clay of each base. The robes simply stately buildings and the bases connotate mossy rock. It's as if the Lohans were designed to sit in a temple or a cave.

Structural Supports: Internal iron armatures were used as supports for the clay. Now they are partially rusted away.

Types and Ages of Beings Represented: All men, from about 25 years of age to perhaps 70 years of age or more, with various psychological dispositions.

Dress: From the evidence of the artist's facility in rendering different ways of wearing monastic clothing, he probably had knowledge of monastic dress codes. He shows different styles of wearing three layers of clothing within the context of vows of an order, representing different degrees of monastic vows by the manner in which the layers of clothing are worn. The Lohans are dressed as legendary individuals in a living system where vows are taken in support of awakening.

Location

	Location
Lohan One:	British Museum, London, p. 3, 5, 42
Lohan Two:	Metropolitan Museum of Art, New York City, p. 6, 9, 34
Lohan Three:	University of Pennsylvania Museum Philadelphia, PA p. 11, 12, 41
Lohan Four:	Nelson-Atkins Museum, Kansas City, p. 15, 16
Lohan Five:	Formely Fuld Collection, Frankfurt-am-mein. In Berlin prior to WWII, now missing and probably destroyed. Complete head, shoulders, and upper chest fragment, p. 18,19
Lohan Six:	Metropolitan Museum of Art, New York City, (head probably not original) p. 21
Lohan Seven:	Museum of Fine Arts, Boston, (head probably not original) p. 22
Lohan Eight:	Royal Ontario Museum, Toronto, (head probably not original) p. 25.

Of the original set of 16 or 18 statues called "The Lohans from I-Chou" the bodies and bases of seven statues remain, four with original heads. There was one magnificent bust that belonged to this group. It was in Berlin before WWII but was missing when the war was over. Three of the surviving statues of the set – Six, Seven and Eight – appear to no longer have their original heads.

Dates

Shakyamuni Buddha	563 - 483 BC.
First Period of Gandharan Art	1st & 2nd C. AD.
Second Period of Ghandharan Art	4th C. AD to 465 AD.
Kumarajiva in China	401 to 413 AD.
Wei unification of northern China, commissioning of Buddhist buildings and Buddhist works of art on a grand scale.	from 460 AD.
Bodhidharma in Northern Wei, China	520 AD.
Huan Tsang's return to China	645 AD.
Sixth and last Ch'an Patriarch	638 to 713 AD.
Chan master Pai Chang	720 to 814 AD.
T'ang Dynasty	618 to 907 AD.
Kuan Hsiu's 16 Lohans	late 9th C AD.
The I-Chou Lohans (Liao)	916 - 1125 C AD.
Southern Song Dynasty	907-1125 C AD.
The Ling-Yan-Si Lohans (Ming)	1368 - 1644 C AD.

Illustration Credits

Pages 3, 4, 31, 42	LOHAN ONE. Courtesy of Robert Newman.
Pages 6, 9, 35	LOHAN TWO. Courtesy of Robert Newman and Tono Hixon. The Metropolitan Museum of Art, New York, NY.
Pages 11,12, 41	LOHAN THREE. Courtesy University of Pennsylvania Museum of Archeology and Anthropology, Philadelphia, PA. Recent conservation and cleaning of this lohan has altered its appearance. Photos courtesy Robert Newman and Tono Hixon.
Pages 15, 16, 27, 32	LOHAN FOUR. Courtesy of Robert Newman and Tono Hixon. The Nelson-Atkins Museum of Art, Kansas City, MO (Purchase: Nelson Trust) 34-6.
Page 18, 37	LOHAN FIVE. After appearing in the Fuld Collection, Frankfort-am-main, Germany, just before WWII, it was in Berlin when the War began,. and was probably destroyed.
Page 21	LOHAN SIX. Courtesy of Robert Newman and Tono Hixon. The Metropolitan Museum of Art, New York, NY.
Page 22	LOHAN SEVEN. Courtesy of the Museum of Fine Arts, Boston. Reproduced with permission. © 2000. All rights reserved.
Page 25	LOHAN EIGHT. Courtesy of the Royal Ontario Museum, Toronto, Canada © ROM

Pages 60, 76, 77	*The Arts Of China*, Michael Sullivan, University of California Press, Berkeley, CA, 1979; pages 109 and 153 (fig. 113 and 167) courtesy of Dr. Michael Sullivan; page 130 (fig. 140) courtesy of John Service.
Page 79	Bodhidharma, Courtesy the Metropolitan Museum of Art, New York, NY. Gift of Mrs Winthrop W. Whitehouse, Mrs. Arnold Whitridge, and Mrs. Sheldon Whitehouse, 1963.
Page 67	Bamiyan, courtesy of Vollker Thewalt.
Pages 28, 29	Bhutanese thanka paintings of Disciples of the Buddha, courtesy of Mathieu Richard.
Page 66	*Buddhist Monuments,* Debala Mitra,1966, plate 88. Courtesy Shishu Sahitya Samsad, Ltd., Calcutta, India.
Pages 56, 57, 58	*China, Der Tempel Gau*, Melckers, Die Louhan von Ling-Yan-Si, Folkwang-verlag, G.M.B.H., Hagen, Germany, 1922
Pages 54, 55, 59	*Chinese Buddhist Monasteries*, J. Prip-Moller, University of Hong Kong Press, 1982; p.37,103, and 232. 1922
Pages 70, 74	*Gandharan Art In Pakistan*, Lyons and Ingholt, Pantheon Books, 1957: plates 52, and 245. Courtesy Mr Lyons.
Page 73	Gandharan Buddha. Courtesy of Moke Mokotoff, Asian Arts, New York, NY

Page 45, 82	*Genshoku Nihon no bijutsu*, Priest Mangan, vol. 21, 1966, pl. 7, p. 15. Priest Eison, no. 86, 7/73. Courtesy of Shogakukan, Inc., Tokyo, Japan
Pages 48-49, 50-51	Liang Kai, 2 paintings, Shanghai Museum. Courtesy the Cultural Relics Publishing House, Beijing, China.
Pages 46, 63	Lohans, Kuan-Hsiu, courtesy of The Imperial Household Agency, Tokyo, Japan.
Page 80	*The Pelican History of Art,* The Art and Architecture of Japan, Paine-Soper, Penguin Books, London, 1955, plate 19.
Pages 53, 62	*The Tun-Huang Caves,* 1990, Courtesy the Cultural Relics Publishing House, Beijing, China.

Acknowledgements

In 1970, after two years of research, photography, and writing, I showed some of the Disciple photographs to the Buddhist meditation master, Chögyam Trungpa. I was ready to drop the project, realizing how naive the effort had been. Rinpoche encouraged me to continue and he promised to help. I had become his student. The Lohans began to reveal their meanings as I engaged in practices of meditation visible in the statues. This work exists largely because of Trungpa Rinpoche's encouragement and his introduction to the book. Some of these lohan photographs, enlarged and printed on silk banners, are used in the Shambhala Training Program, created by Trungpa Rinpoche to introduce the sitting practice of meditation to a wide audience.

Also in 1970, while using the research facilities of the NYU Fine Arts Institute, I met Professor Alexander Soper, who proved to be another vital support. He was chairman of the Asian Studies Department of NYU, had traveled in China, knew the Chinese language well, and had done research in Chinese Buddhist art. He saw me as a kind of determined free bird going into a research area that needed work, giving me encouragement and substantial assistance. He brought to the project his own sensitivity to spiritual art and academic credibility. He was helpful for years.

In the summer of 1974, in Boulder, Colorado, in the context of Naropa Institute where we were both teaching, I met Deborah Salter-Klimborg, an art historian and a Buddhist who was married to the director of the Asian Arts Institute in Kabul, Afghanistan. She lived near the region of what was once Gandhara. Her feedback was helpful for my understanding of the development of Buddhist imagery in Gandhara.

Some of this work was featured in LOKA, the first publication of Naropa Institute, October 1975.* Rick Fields, editor-in-chief, was very helpful in the editing of seven pages of photos and writing for that publication.

Francesca Fremantle was of help in more ways than one. She transcribed the spoken introduction with Trungpa Rinpoche and gave encouragement to the work on this book.

In 1980, in New York City, I met His Holiness Dudjom Rinpoche, head of the Nyingma lineage of Tibetan Vajrayana Buddhism. I continued my practice and study with him and his son Shenphen Dawa Rinpoche. I am extremely grateful to be able to present "The Torch of Precious Jewels: A Sadhana of the Buddha and the Sixteen Arhats" by Dudjom Rinpoche, translated by the Padmakara Translation Group at Chanteloube, France, 1986. The Tibetan woodblock prints of the arhats were directed by Dudjom Rinpoche. We have also included two arhat thankas photographed by Matheiu Ricard in Bhutan.

Carolyn Rose Gimian, Chögyam Trungpa's editor, helped us finalize the presentation of his language. We are very grateful to Mrs. Diana J. Mukpo for allowing us to use Chögyam Trungpa's commentary on the lohan statues.

From the very beginning and throughout, Mr. William Segal of the Gurdjieff Foundation was helpful and supportive. James George has been helpful for many years. I have much gratitude to Tej Hazarika, the publisher of Cool Grove Press, for all his patient work in preparing this book for publication and Loren Standlee for production assistance and support.

---

* LOKA; A journal from the Naropa Institute, Anchor Press/Doubleday, Garden City, NY. "Anchor Books edition 1975" ISBN: 0-385-02312-X. Library of Congress Catalog Card Number 74-31515. Copyright 1975 by Nalanda Foundation/Naropa Institute."The I-Chou Lohans and the Stages of Realization. P 114-120

Brief Biographical Sketches

Considered to be the direct representative of Padmasambhava in our time, His Holiness Dudjom Rinpoche (1908-1987) born in Tibet, wrote twenty-three volumes of revealed teachings. He gathered and corrected all the Kama teachings of the Nyingmapa lineage. Dudjom Rinpoche established numerous monasteries and meditation centers throughout the world after leaving Tibet.

Born in Tibet in 1939, Chögyam Trungpa was recognized in infancy as the reincarnate abbot of the surmang group of monasteries. He came to North America in the early 1970 and over the next fifteen years founded a network of several hundred Buddhist meditation centers throughout the United States and Canada. He also established the first Buddhist-inspired university in North America, The Naropa University in Boulder, Colorado. Chögyam Trungpa was also an artist and a poet. Many artists—poets, playwrights, painters, photographers, dancers and others were drawn to study with him or to teach at Naropa.

Robert Newman has taught at the City University of New York, Naropa University and the University of Colorado. He is the founder and president of the World Health Foundation which has developed programs for the medical uses of meditation now offered in hospitals and medical centers. His book, Calm Birth will be published in Fall 2001; (www.Medigrace.org).

Note from the Publisher

This book would not have come together without the help and support of Loren Standlee, Arthur Mandelbaum, Jeff Kleinbard, Tim Marion, James George, Murad Heerjee, and Robert Newman's unshakable faith in the feasibility of such a project.
All praises due to the myriads of immortals, all Tathaghatas—conquerors of the armies of error and ignorance.